Tougher Than Woodpecker Lips

By

AL RUDOLPH

Acknowledgements

I want to thank my wife, Linda, for her encouragement and support, not only through the writing of this book, but for the love she has shown me for the past 39 years. She was the driving force in my coming to accept the Lord, and she has been there for me even when I did not deserve it. Linda truly is the wind beneath my wings.

I am also eternally grateful to our daughter, Stephanie, for always believing in me, and for her adventuresome spirit. She helps me see the good in others and in life, and for that, I am most grateful.

This project would not have been possible without the help of my assistant, Mary Marshall, who took care of business so I could get to the business of writing. She is the best.

This being my first attempt at writing, I am forever thankful to Randy West, for his skill at editing my thoughts and making them a bit more palatable to you, the reader. In addition, without the technical assistance I received from Chris Graves, I would still be struggling with getting the manuscript ready for print. I also appreciate the artistic gifts of Joy Murdoch, who was instrumental in designing the front cover.

Last, but definitely not least, heartfelt thanks to my dear friends, Steve and Carolyn Wood, who allowed me to live in their beautiful home in Saltillo, Tennessee, while I wrote these words. This is just an example of the generosity and love they have for so many. Steve and Carolyn, I am forever in your debt.

Table of Contents

꒦꒷꒦

Introduction

I cannot remember when or from whom I first heard the phrase *"Tougher than woodpecker lips,"* but I do know it was a day in my youth many years ago. I recall thinking at the time that whatever it was that fit this description was something not to be messed with. I took a liking to the saying and stored it in my memory bank, waiting for the right time to put it to use. I believe the time is now.

Through the years, I have watched countless woodpeckers beat their heads against trees with no noticeable harmful side effects - for the woodpecker, anyway. For something to be tougher than the "lips" the birds used to pound with (actually make holes in the bark), they had to be pretty tough indeed. It occurred to me one day as I was talking to a friend that life itself is sometimes *"Tougher than woodpecker lips,"* and if we hope to survive, we must be tougher still and possess certain traits in our character to stand up against whatever the world throws our way.

In the pages that follow, I touch on forty different subjects that I believe are important to all who try to live their lives to the best of their ability. Most of the issues I have written about are of the positive nature and need to be made a part of our everyday living. However, a small number of the chapters deal with things that we should be aware of, just to make sure they don't take up permanent residence in our life.

I hope you enjoy reading these chapters as much as I enjoyed writing them, and if you are made better from something herein, then praise be to our Lord, Jesus Christ. For these writings are thoughts He blessed me with, and I pray that He uses them to bless you, too. Take hope in the fact that life may be tough, but you can be *"Tougher than woodpecker lips"* - and not only survive, but thrive!

Al Rudolph

1 - Believe It, And You Can Achieve It!

W e must not allow our thoughts to hinder our possibilities. It is a fact that if you think you can't, you won't! Each of us has more potential that we ever thought we had, and if we can comprehend that and act upon that belief, we can achieve new heights. Roger Banister, the first man to run a four-minute mile, was not the first man to possess the ability to run a four-minute mile. However, he was evidently the first to truly believe he could. So, do not allow little thinking to prevent you from achieving big. Many times achievement comes by taking a series of small steps instead of giant leaps. If we have the ability to break the large obstacles down into smaller "bite-size" pieces, we can consume much more than anyone thought possible. *"Believe it, and you can achieve it!"*

"We must not allow our thoughts to hinder our possibilities."

We also must be willing to do the things that others are not. When others give up, we must get up. No matter what trials and hardships we might face, no matter how strong the struggle, we have no choice but to persevere.

We cannot allow discouragement to take our eyes off the goal for which we are striving because if we do, we will soon begin to sink.

Our level of achievement is closely related to our ability to overcome the negative. Many will give up at the first sign of hardship, but if we are going to accomplish anything worthwhile, we must not become discouraged. Life is an uphill battle, and one that cannot be won without facing struggles. If we hope to conquer our opposition, we must be willing to make sacrifices. The only road leading to the land of achievement goes up and over the mountain of negativism. Success without hardships is no success at all; it is simply a gift. To achieve more than others, we must be willing to suffer more pain than the others. For gain without pain only comes in the form of luck or an inheritance. No pain, no gain!

Very seldom do you find anyone achieving greatness who is not willing to do more than what is expected of them. It is not the amount of ease but the amount of effort that determines the glory level of any achievement. The highest level of achievement is one in which we have given our all, our best. We may not have succeeded in winning the race, but if we held nothing back, we won! The journey toward achievement is many times more rewarding than the achievement itself.

We must not allow where we are in life to prevent us from going where we wish to be.

Just because we were born into poverty does not mean we should stay there. You can achieve what you can believe! We should not be concerned about *what* we don't have, but *why* we don't have it. Sometimes for achievement to take place, we must think outside the box, and even forget that the box exists. We have to take steps that others are not willing to take, and attempt things that others dare not tackle.

Thomas H. Huxley once said, *"The rung of the ladder was never meant to rest upon, but only to hold a man's foot long enough to enable him to put the other somewhat higher."* The one who rests on what he has done in the past is passed! Former Notre Dame football coach Lou Holtz says, *"If what you did yesterday seems big, you haven't done anything today."*

Three things necessary to accomplish any worthwhile achievement are the willingness to work hard, work long and work smart. Michelangelo said, *"If people knew how hard I worked to get my mastery, it wouldn't seem so wonderful after all."* At the end of our life, if it can be said of us that we did all we could with what we had, we will have achieved success. It is not so important where you end up in life, as it is in how far you have come from where you started. And the amount of opposition you were able to overcome on the way plays a part in the measure of success. The title of "great" was never awarded to one who gave up; it's reserved for those who have persevered.

Achievement in the eyes of the world is no achievement at all if you lose what is most important to you in the experience. The true measure of a person in regard to achievement has to do with the fact that he or she was able to maintain their health and the health of their relationships as they progressed.

In the end, if what you achieve does not better humanity, it hardly can be called a success. When we develop our talents and use them to serve others, we will achieve. If fame is the name of the game you are trying to win, you lose! We should strive to better our own lives plus as many other lives as we possibly can. Then and only then do you become a winner.

"You can achieve what you can believe!"

Your level of dedication will determine your level of achievement. We must break the chains that bind us in mediocrity because we were designed to be better than we are.

We also have to remember that activity does not equal achievement. Just because we are busy all the time does not mean we are actually getting any closer to our goal. Be on guard, and do a regular self-examination to make sure you are growing, not just going. My closing advice for you is simply, *"Believe it and you can achieve it!"*

*****

"To him who overcomes, I will give the right to sit with me on my throne, just as I overcame and sat down with my father on his throne." [Revelation 3:21]

2 - Friend or Foe?

Albert Einstein once said, *"In the middle of every diffi-culty lies opportunity."* That may be true, sometimes hard to see, and even harder to believe when trouble shows up at our door. However, if we will take a look at most of the people who have accomplished great things, we will discover that they endured great adversities. History reveals that what happens *to* a person is not nearly the deciding factor as what happens *within* the person. Each of us will have trouble - that **is** one of the promises of scripture. How we react to it will be a tell tale sign of what we are made of.

"Sometimes the fear of failing prevents us from facing our foes."

To develop our true character we must be able to be beaten and bruised in our bout with life, and yet be unwilling to throw in the towel. We must learn from our mistakes and then take what we learn and apply it in the next battles. For if we learn from our sparring with setbacks to come out swinging, we can win the round and eventually the fight. Sometimes the fear of failing prevents us from facing our foes. No matter how huge they appear, they too will succumb to our steadfast blows. The bigger the battle, the more tremendous the triumph.

Problems are not only a regular at the table of poverty; they are a familiar guest at the best of banquet halls. It has been said, "Into each life a little rain must fall", but the question is, "Will we allow it to dampen our spirits or refresh our reservoir?" All roads will eventually have potholes; the same is true on the streets of life.

Instinct tells us to pack our bags and move out when trouble moves in, but integrity tells us to stay and be the landlord. Without problems, we will never realize our true potential. Sometimes we stand tallest when we are on our knees; whether we are there to praise or plead makes little difference. Trouble trembles when we take time to pray. The times of trials may well be the doorway to the town of Trust. We must resolve that many times we cannot do it alone.

If we will allow them to, our trials can be turning points toward triumph instead of detours toward disaster. Failure is not fatal unless we allow it to consume us in a fire of fury. Step back and take a good look at what we at first identified as a foe; surprisingly, there you may well find a friend. Do not be too swift in saying something is a curse - it could be the cure you have been chasing. Remember, the same breeze that slams the door can fill your sails.

Each of us will face difficult times in our lives. Some of us will "break down," and some will "break through." Adversity aligns itself face-to-face with our attitude.

Whether we become the winner or the whiner is up to us. The times of triumph are not nearly as important in determining the true character of a person as the days of defeat. When disaster strikes, fear normally follows. However, instead of turning tail to run, we should step up to the plate and prepare to hit a home run.

"Adversity aligns itself face to face with our attitude."

Much unhappiness in life is caused by our desire to dodge the bullet and not be concerned about why we were shot at in the first place. Just as surely as hills are made to climb, troubles are made to test the make-up of our character. Odds are that the more you understand the truth that problems can be possibilities in disguise, the more likely you are to tackle them head on and see the potential that each holds. Ironically, sometimes when adversity strikes, we need to take a break and let it attempt to resolve itself. Even if it does not, the refresher may allow us to see it from a different perspective, and come away with a new approach to an old problem. Look at each time you try as a learning situation, and come away stronger for having fought the battle.

Take the time to look for the "oil" in the turmoil's of life. It may be just what you need to keep you from squeaking about your troubles. If we search diligently enough we can find at least some good in the worst of conditions.

Also, adversity has a way of enabling us get to know ourselves. True leaders are those who have learned how to achieve new levels of accomplishment by making the most of difficult times. Instead of allowing disappointments to damper the spirit, use them to envision and enlighten.

The Chinese symbol for crisis has a dual meaning: danger and opportunity. When crisis comes calling, we need to do our best to remember that with the pain come possibilities. My wish for you is to minimize the pain and magnify the potential.

*****

"Though I walk in the midst of trouble, you preserve my life; you stretch out your hand against the anger of my foes, with your right hand you save me." [Psalm 138:7]

3 - Is The Gain Worth The Pain?

Have you ever known someone who seemed as if they were mad at the whole world? They act as if their task in life is to struggle under the weight from the chip on their shoulder. When I think of someone like that, I have to ask myself, *"Is the gain worth the pain?"* I believe that any gain that comes from being angry is so minute that it is never worth the pain that comes afterward. The pain comes not only from outside sources but also from within ourselves when we fail to control our emotions and let anger take over the throne of our senses.

It takes little or no effort to become angry and upset. The hard part is knowing whom to be angry with, how much anger is just the right amount, and what is the best way to express it? To truly have control of our anger, we must not only control the words we say, but also control our actions and the tone of our voice that accompany our words. Before you allow your emotions to take control, and you choose to let anger speak your mind, remember to think how your words will sound to others, and the damage they may do to those within hearing distance.

"It takes little or no effort to become angry and upset."

It is far better to control your anger and retain the respect of others than to lose control and lose respect. Uncontrolled anger is like a loose cannon - you never know where the next shot is going! Losing your temper means losing one of your most treasured assets. Guard it closely!

Before we take the liberty of giving someone a piece of our mind, it would be wise to take a quick inventory just to make sure we have enough to spare. To have conquered the enemy called anger is to have prevented many battles from ever taking place, and to have won a major war. Throwing words of anger at someone is akin to throwing rocks at a person. One leaves cuts and bruises to the body, the other to the heart and soul. If we do not learn how to control our anger, it won't be long until we discover that our anger is controlling us.

Before you allow your anger to be displayed in public, make sure the public will benefit from seeing it. If not, keep it behind closed doors and locked away, for your own good. Angry men are blind to the destructive power of their words; too bad they aren't mute as well! Before we allow anger to slide over into the driver's seat and take control of our emotions, we need to consider what the consequences of "reckless driving" may be.

People are not like water because each of us has a different boiling point. The toughest part is knowing what that point is for each person you meet, and making sure you turn down the heat before they reach it. We can easily come up with a bucket full of reasons to condone our anger, but will any of them hold water?

To become angry is to become like an animal that reacts in such a way to snarl and pounce before considering the size of the enemy. When this happens, it often bites off more than it can chew. To be angry is to be momentarily insane.

"To be angry is to be momentarily insane."

When we react in anger, we are not content with just getting even with our oppressor, we always want to go one better. The question then becomes, "Where does it end?" In times like this, we need to accept the role of being more mature and decide not to retaliate but to retreat. Have you ever noticed the phenomenon that takes place when a man closes his hands to make fists with which to fight? His brain closes up as well.

One who is quick to become angry is a fool; one who has self-control and has his anger reined in, is wise. Many times anger is used in place of knowledge. If we don't know something, often, for no good reason, we become upset, first with ourselves, and then with others. In a like manner, when a person is wrong, but not big enough to admit it, they, too, usually react in fits of anger. John K. Morley once said, *"The size of the man can be measured by the size of what it takes to make him angry."*

A mean-spirited person has a terrible disease that can only be cured by a change of heart.

If you don't want to be angry, then don't! The choice is yours. You must give me the right to make you mad before I can do so. It is better not to act in moments of anger, for to do so will bring you hours of sorrow. When angry, count to ten. If you are still angry, but have contained your anger, count your blessings.

"We cannot throw darts of anger at someone else without some becoming boomerangs and returning home."

We cannot throw darts of anger at someone else without some becoming boomerangs and returning home. To waste part of our life in fits of unrighteous anger is to forfeit time that could have been used for something much more honorable.

Who among us has not been angry with themselves for being angry? If we can learn to control our anger, we will save ourselves a tremendous amount of heartache. However, when a person becomes angry with himself or herself because they lost control of their anger, this is a sign of hope. In each incidence where anger is a possibility, we must ask ourselves, *"Is the gain worth the pain?"*

*****

"My dear brothers, take note of this: Everyone should be quick to listen, slow to speak and slow to become angry, for man's anger does not bring about the righteous life that God desires." [James 1:19-20]

4 - Attitude Adjustment

I have concluded that "Attitude" is nothing more than a "mind game". We all get playing time, and nothing plays a more important part in shaping our lives than how we play the game. The score is kept a bit differently though, because the emphasis is more on assists than in points scored. The truth is, that you are the only one keeping track of those. If you are observant, you will realize that some people seem to foul out of every game while others seldom do. The only spectators are the other players, and everyone is a referee of sorts. It should be good news for each of us that every game is played on our home court. This can be a huge advantage or a similarly large disadvantage - it all depends on the material you used in the construction of your playing floor. It is time for you to check into the game. So go make yourself proud!

"How each of us views our circumstances packs more punch than the circumstances themselves."

The importance of your outside circumstances stands as a dwarf in comparison to the gigantic proportions of your attitude. How each of us views our circumstances packs more punch than the circumstances themselves. More often than not, we knock ourselves out.

The face of the fact before us plays a small part in what we see. Our sight is determined by the quality of our eyes. In Luke 11:34 Jesus says, *"Your eye is the lamp of your body. When your eyes are good, your whole body is full of light. But when they are bad, your whole body also is full of darkness."* If your outlook on life has been a bit faded lately, it could be that you need an "I" exam.

We have a tendency to sort experiences into categories of good and bad, when a more appropriate grading would be good and not quite so good. The language we use when talking to ourselves is just as important, if not more so, than what others say to us. We must make sure that optimism is our mother tongue.

"Sticks and stones may break my bones, but words may never hurt me." If you can honestly say this, then you are in control of your attitude, and the world tips its hat at you and says "Congratulations."

It is amazing how quickly life can turn on you. One minute you are driving down "Easy Street," and the next you are on "Awful Avenue." Fact is, you are behind the wheel, and you alone make the decision to continue in the direction you are going - or take the next exit and get back on course. Which way are you headed?

"We must make sure optimism is our native tongue."

Salt and pepper are both seasonings for our food, but each brings a unique taste. The same is true for the good and bad attitudes that we allow to flavor our "food for thought." Your mental taste buds will determine not only how good you and others feel when they are around you, but also the degree of sickness we might feel. If something that we are eating doesn't taste good to us, our natural response is to spit it out. Shouldn't we do the same thing in our minds?

In case you haven't noticed, the world is quick to applaud winners, and just as swift to appease whiners. The great news is that each of us gets to choose into which corner we will step.

The "winds of life" will blow against us all. Whether we bend and break under the pressure, or grow stronger from the resistance will determine whether we end up as building material or simply as sticks that cause others to stumble and fall.

A man walked through a store one day and spotted a guitar for sale. Being untrained and unskilled in guitar playing, it is no wonder that all he heard when he strummed the strings was noise. He had not walked more than a few feet away when his ears perked up to a familiar tune that was coming from behind him. It was music to his ears. He turned to see that someone else, much more skilled than himself, had picked up the same guitar and played it well. For him to have blamed the guitar for the different results would be just as silly as someone trying to blame the circumstances of the world for their unaccomplished life. Our perception and opinion of what happens to us always has the final word.

Your circumstances are like a wild stallion over which you have no restraints. Your attitude is like that of a gentle riding horse; you are in the saddle and have full control of the reins.

True bankruptcy occurs only in our mental banks, but that in turn is tied ever so tightly to our wealth in the world.

Film producer Mike Todd once said, *"I've never been poor, only broke. Being poor is a frame of mind. Being broke is only a temporary situation."* The next time you find yourself thinking "poor little old me," stop and make a deposit! As a matter of fact, make a complete *attitude adjustment*.

*****

"Your attitude should be the same as that of Jesus Christ." [Philippians 2:5]

5 - Do You Need Any Change?

On a recent visit to one of the local restaurants, I went to pay my $12.50 lunch tab with a $100 bill. When the waiter picked up the folder with my check and money (in plain sight) in it, he had the nerve to ask, *"Do you need any change?"* Being the quick thinker I am, I answered, "Yes, please." As he walked away, my first thought was, what an absurd question to ask a tightwad like me. Of course I need change! Then it dawned on me that he might be a psychology major, and he may have really been asking me if I needed to make any change in my *life*. If that happens to be the case, my answer is still the same, "Yes, please." And I would have to add, "Of course I need change!" Who among us wouldn't answer the same?

> ***"Change is the only constant in our ever-changing world."***

When you get to the point in life that you decide you are not going to change, then I might say, "It's been good knowing you!" If you become complacent and hesitant to change, you might as well make arrangements with the local funeral parlor, because you are dead! Change is the only constant in our ever-changing world. For one who is not willing to change his or her mind, they must be content with changing nothing.

If we are unwilling to change, we must be content with our lot in life - and expect it to grow worse everyday. To change means we have new opportunities ahead of us, and it allows us a chance to make sure our focus is where it needs to be. Sometimes the path of least resistance is the one where we ask someone else to change, and we remain steadfast; at least as much as possible, for even when we try our best not to change, we change. If one is willing to make changes in his own life first, he has a much greater chance of convincing his neighbor to do the same. If we come to realize just how hesitant we are to change ourselves, it will help us be more tolerant of others when they hesitate.

Preston Bradley said, *"I've never met a person - I don't care what his condition - in whom I could not see possibilities. I don't care how much a man may consider himself a failure, I believe in him, for he can change the thing that is wrong in his life any time he is ready and prepared to do it. Whenever he develops the desire, he can take away from his life the thing that is defeating it. The capacity for reformation and change lies within."* Each of us has the capacity to change, but the tough part is getting to the point of being ready and prepared to make the change. Within each of us are small things that we can change that would offer huge rewards. It is the uncertain effects of change that makes people hesitate.

What is real today may be unreal tomorrow, and what is real tomorrow may be unreal today. For no matter how hard we try to be ready for change, we can never foresee what will be required for tomorrow. If it were not for change this life would become unbelievably boring in such a short time. Unless we are constantly attempting to make things better, they will get worse on their own. If only we could get a glimpse of what change was bringing with it, we would be much more comfortable. There are no changes that last forever because they are forever changing!

"Unless we are constantly attempting to make things better, they will get worse on their own."

If you continue to do things the way you have always done them and expect the outcome to be different, you are only fooling yourself. Change makes the difference. Far too often we are not willing to risk what we are, for what we have the possibility of becoming. Change your mind about changing!

To remain young has more to do with your willingness to change and try new things than it does with elixirs and cold creams. People will spend their life savings trying to slow life down, while all they really need to do is to embrace change and refuse to allow it to make you old before your time. Times change, and it's really a blessing that we change as well. We must respect the past but look to the future with anticipation and reverence.

Change sometimes causes pain, but the old adage, *"No pain, no gain,"* is right on in this regard. Too often we attempt to make changes to our world when we should be making changes within. To change the world, start with yourself!

It is not the fact that things change so quickly that causes most of the anxiety and worry; it is the fact that we are so slow in adapting. The thing that makes change so exciting is the possibilities that come with it. Just when we feel like we finally have things all figured out, they change. Such is life!

"To change the world, start with yourself!"

To take down a fence without finding out why it was built in the first place is foolishness. However, if you should discover that the original reason for building it no longer exists, grab the sledge hammer! If the time is right for a change, do yourself a favor and welcome it. An old Turkish proverb says, *"No matter how far you have gone on a wrong road, turn back."* Once again, if the time is right for a change, be willing to let it happen without resisting it. I will close this chapter by asking, *"Do you need any change?"*

*****

"Why do you look at the speck of sawdust in your brother's eye and pay no attention to the plank in your own eye? How can you say to your brother, 'Brother, let me take the speck out of your eye,' when you yourself fail to see the plank in your own eye? You hypocrite, first take the plank out of your own eye, and then you will see clearly to remove the speck from your brothers eye." Luke 6:41-42

6 - The Choice Is Yours!

Choices. So many choices! Our lives are what they are because of the choices we have made up to this point. Little choices, like what to wear, what to eat, or what to say. Big choices, like what to do for work, whom to marry, where to live. Our daily lives are filled up with making choices. Some of the ones we considered little choices at the time end up having big consequences. Let's take, for instance, what to eat. It is a proven fact that our overall health is determined by the food we eat, and many of the diseases that plague us today are the result of choices we made in the past. Countless millions of people today wish they had made different choices when it came to deciding what to eat. This is just one small example of how the choices we make today determine the lives we live tomorrow. All of us wish we had made different choices. However, we cannot change those decisions, but we can learn from our mistakes and make wiser decisions in the future. If hindsight and foresight could change places, we would all make different choices. You are the captain of your ship, and the decisions you make through rough water and the smooth sailing alike will determine in which port you end up. *"The choice is yours!"* May you choose wisely.

"If hindsight and foresight could change places, we would all make different choices."

The making of choices is the most important thing each of us does on a daily basis, and yet most are made without an inkling as to what the results will be. Making choices solely on what "feels good" will usually end up with results that "feel bad." This freedom of choice determines everything about you: who you will be, what you will have, who your friends are, and what you will do for a living, just to name a few. We have no right to be mad at the world for what our lives hold for us because, in most cases, it is exactly what we have chosen.

The true measure of a person is determined by what he or she does when they are completely free to choose. In such times, the natural tendency is to consider what would make the "self" most happy. However, it would behoove the chooser to think about what would make other lives more pleasant, and choose that path. The choices made with selfish motives often carry the greatest penalty.

The direction in which you choose to travel will most likely determine where you end up. You may one day ask yourself, "How in the world did my life get to be such a mess?" and the answer is, "By the choices you made!" Before making a major choice, gather as many facts as possible, and then be willing to accept responsibility for any decision you make, based on the facts you have.

Understand going in that all the facts you have may not be all the facts there are, and that some of the "facts" you have are not facts at all. But the key here is to be willing to claim responsibility for the consequences, and not blame others for the way things turns out.

Our lives are not so much like a train ride that has the exact path laid out for us but more like a cross-country hike on which we choose what path we wish to walk. Sometimes the best route to choose is not the one that appears to be the smoothest and most traveled but the one few others are willing to try. To receive what you want, you first must decide exactly what that is, and then choose, to the best of your ability, the path that will lead you there in the most efficient manner. The greatest power anyone has is the power to choose his or her path in life.

You have the power to do what you want to do and be what you want to be. The question is, "Are you willing to accept the fact that you will have to make choices, and be ready to accept the consequences, and make sacrifices along the way?" Each of us holds the key to our life in the choices we make. You are the keeper of the "master key" that will unlock each door to the storehouse of your choosing. Some will unlock worlds of beauty and blessings, others will forever be bound with burdens. The beauty of it is, if you don't like what you see when you look in the mirror, you and you alone can make the choices to beautify the image. Realizing that you alone have complete control of your thoughts helps you to understand that you alone have the deciding vote in your destiny. The world serves up both good and bad, but the choice is ours as to which we choose. To be in complete control of your thoughts makes you the most powerful person in your life.

> *"Each of us holds the key to our life in the choices we make."*

Imagine that you are the Master Gardener, and you decide whether weeds or flowers adorn your lot. So it is with your life. Many times people will offer excuses for the way things are, but they really need to understand that the way things are is because of the choices they made. The freedom of choice can be a blessing or a curse, depending on what choices you make. When faced with a fork in the road of life, choose wisely which you take because once you choose, your choices now control you.

If you are not happy with your current circumstances, then make the decision to change what you can, and change the way you look at the ones you cannot alter. Then get ready to live. The question is not, "Will you do it for me?" the question is, "Will you do it for yourself?" *The choice is yours!*

*****

"How much better to get wisdom than gold, to choose understanding rather than silver." [Proverbs 16:16]

7 - Are You In or Out?

A doctor was making his rounds at the local mental hospital when he noticed a patient with his ear to the wall. The doctor asked what was going on. The patient says, "Shhhhh. Listen!" So now, the doctor has his ear to the wall. After a few seconds, he says, "I don't hear anything." The patient says, "I know. It's been that way all morning!"

Now you might say that someone like that needs to be committed, and I agree a hundred percent. But I also believe that you need to be committed as well! Maybe not to an institution, but to making the most of the talents you have been blessed with.

One of my favorite quotes in regards to commitment is from Kenneth Blanchard, and it is, *"There's a difference between interest and commitment. When you are interested in doing something, you do it only when it's convenient. When you are committed to something, you accept no excuses, only results."* Commitment means getting up every time you are knocked down, and letting the opponent know that you aren't going anywhere. Peak performance is the result of complete commitment.

"Peak performance is the result of complete commitment."

Commitment means training for and competing in a marathon, not going around the block for a walk. What you commit yourself to become, you will be. Starting any task is the job half-done; commitment makes up the other three-fourths!

Commit to be the best, whether it is the best janitor, salesperson, teacher, factory worker, etc. It does not matter, for even the lowest of positions with commitment will contribute more to this world than a lofty position laced with laziness.

If you think something is worth doing, then do something! The four words, "One of these days," hinders dreams from ever becoming reality. Start with what you have, where you are, and someday soon you will arrive at the door of success with your arms full of accomplishments. Success is more the result of a person being committed than natural ability. Gifted individuals who are not driven to develop and use their talents will take them to their grave. Many accomplishments have been the result of a common person with an uncommon drive.

I am reminded of what real commitment looks like when I remember that Michelangelo was left almost blind from the paint that had dripped into his eyes while he painted the Sistine Chapel. That is total commitment, and the results have awed audiences ever since. You and you alone are the one who paints your portrait on the canvas of life. Will it be a treasured masterpiece or yard sale quality? Total commitment enables a person to succeed at levels others never even consider.

When a goal is kidnapped by commitment, the reward of seeing it come home far outweighs any ransom paid. Commitment will allow one to be courageous, calm and confrontational when it is necessary. Lou Holtz said, *"If you don't make a total commitment to whatever you're doing, then you start looking to bail out the first time the boat starts leaking. It's tough enough to get the boat to shore with everybody rowing, let alone when a guy stands up and starts putting his life jacket on."* You will have a tough time convincing others to take up arms with you and join the battle when you are A.W.O.L. Nothing brings death more rapidly to a dream than an owner who is not willing to die for it.

"Excuses are what make an able bodied person walk with a limp."

To lead in times of plenty is a breeze. To come alongside of in times of conflict means facing the winds of opposition. To get behind and push during all-out war is standing strong in the eye of the storm. Those who will not give their "whole" self will soon find that they live in the "hole" most of the time. Commitment and accomplishments are always found hanging out together. For those who are not committed, defeat comes quickly. However, when commitment closes and locks all the doors so excuses cannot enter, it is safe.

Excuses are what make an able-bodied person walk with a limp.

Find your dream and then hold fast to it, as if your life and livelihood depend on it, because they do. Remember the old saying, "It is better to be a 'has-been' than a 'never-was'." The only question left for you to answer now is, *"Are you in or out?"*

*****

> *"We hear that some among you are idle. They are not busy; they are busybodies. Such people we command and urge in the Lord Jesus Christ to settle down and earn the bread they eat. And as for you, brothers, never tire of doing what is right."* [2 Thessalonians 3:11-13]

8 - Bring It On, Bubba!

Have you ever found yourself in a situation where you wanted to stand up and say, *"Bring it on, Bubba!"* but ended up staying seated and whispering to yourself, "I want no part of this."? I am sure all of us have, and we end up kicking ourselves because we just didn't seem to have the confidence we wished we had. Confidence is a tricky thing, and if it ends up being based on thoughts that are not true, and therefore instills in us a false courage, it can end up getting us whipped by all the Bubbas in life. Sometimes, confidence is nothing more than ignorance dressed up as bravery. On the other hand, if we have prepared and done our homework, the test at hand should be of little or no concern. We must have confidence in ourselves to find our true place in the world and fulfill our reason for living. Having that confidence also allows us not to worry about what others may think but to continue doing our best.

The degree of confidence that others have in you will determine how willing they are to believe and trust in you in all their dealings with you. Moreover, the degree of confidence you have in yourself will many times be a determining factor in others level of confidence in you as well. However, we must be careful and not allow our confidence to turn into conceit. For conceit is a weird disease that makes everyone sick except the one who has it. Self-confidence knows how to control itself and is not to be confused with conceit. Conceit is a feeling of superiority and self-importance; it shows no signs of modesty. Our confidence we have in ourselves should never exceed our ability. If and when it does, prepare for a crash landing.

> *"Our confidence we have in ourselves should never exceed the ability we posses."*

Confidence just doesn't magically appear out of thin air. It comes from hours, days, weeks, months and years of practicing the trick until you are sure of your ability to perform. Confidence breeds courage. Together the two make a family that gets things done.

John Dewey once said, *"Confidence...is directness and courage in meeting the facts of life."* I would say that the confidence must be accompanied by a willingness to accept either the consequences or the congratulations, depending on the outcome of the situation.

Confidence enables us to do things we never thought we could, using power we never knew we had. Confidence gives our hope and trust a place to live. Never doubt yourself, for when you do, you shut off all sources of creative energy and therefore limit your productivity. It is a truth that life is not always easy for any of us, but if we will persevere and believe in ourselves, we can overcome and grow from our trials.

Many times we defeat ourselves before we ever face our opponent because of our lack of confidence. If we ever hope to win, we must first believe we can! If we don't have the confidence that our ability is up to the task at hand, we are behind before we even start. A right confidence in yourself can and will instill doubt in any opposition you may face.

Our confidence should be the result of preparation, not dependent on the presentation. We should allow every small victory to play its part in giving us the confidence needed to tackle what others consider impossible. Do what you do the best you can, and treat others in a way you wish to be treated, and you can have confidence in the result. You must prepare to have confidence, to have confidence!

Believing in and having confidence in another will be more helpful to them than any physical strength you might lend them. For if we show confidence in others, they are likely to repay the favor. On the other hand, if you fail to have confidence in another, it is difficult to fully regain their respect in the future. For our lack of confidence in them leads them to have a lack of confidence in us, and so it goes. When you lose confidence, you lose so much more than that!

It is hard to instill confidence in the lives of others in regards to something that you yourself see little or no value in. If you do not believe something is worth the energy, those under your leadership will soon come to the same conclusion.

Confidence and enthusiasm together can climb almost any mountain. We must never allow worry and doubt to drive our lives, for they will always lead us to dead-end streets.

> *"Confidence and enthusiasm can climb almost any mountain when they are together."*

The person who has the confidence to continue marching forward in the face of criticism is either fortunate or a fruitcake; it all depends on the size of the opposition, and on how well they have prepared to fight. You know the old saying, "It doesn't matter about the size of the dog in the fight; it depends on the size of the fight in the dog!" So, go ahead, I believe in you; stand up and say, *"Bring it on, Bubba!"* Just be sure you have your running shoes on when you say it.

*****

"So do not throw away your confidence; it will be richly rewarded." [Hebrews 10:35]

9 - Nope, But I Have Always Wanted To!

How much better would the world be if we would just cooperate with each other and try to see the situation through the eyes of those who are in opposition to us? Sometimes we just need to be convinced that the best thing to do is simply cooperate with one another. I love the story that is told from the days of the Gold Rush, and the little green horn prospector who showed up, ready to strike it rich. Before getting on the trail to the gold fields, he decided to stop in the local saloon and have himself a drink. As he bellied up to the bar, a big burly guy from Texas pulled up along side of him and said, *"You look like a city slicker to me, son. Where you from?"* The little fella answered, *"Boston, and I have come to stake my claim."* The Texan asked, *"Did you ever learn to dance back there?"* The Bostonian admitted that he had not. So the Texan pulled his pistol from his holster and said, *"Well, I am going to teach you how!"* He began to shoot at the little guy's feet, causing him to hop, skip and jump all the way out the door, where he was shaking like a leaf.

About an hour later, as the Texan was walking out the doors of the saloon, he heard a distinct click. He turned to look and found himself some three feet from the end of the biggest shotgun he had ever seen, held by the little prospector. The next thing he heard was the voice of the little prospector asking, *"Hey, mister, did you ever kiss a mule's butt?"* The quick thinking Texan answered, *"Nope, but I have always wanted to!"*

May you always be in the cooperative mode, for you never know when your life is going to depend on it.

"Our success will be closely linked to our level of cooperation."

Cooperation carries with it an attitude of help and support, through which we are able to satisfy the wants of the day. Our success will be closely linked to our level of cooperation. When others see and understand that you are agreeable and easy to work with, they will do whatever they can to help. When we join our efforts with the efforts of others, things begin to happen and mountains move.

If you can appeal to the hearts of others, they will be more than willing to lend you a hand - and often even help finance the project. Success is determined by the fact that you cooperate with, and use, but never abuse, others to help you achieve your goals. As long as the tune you are singing is in harmony with those around you, the world is a happier and more happening place.

Relationships will not develop unless everyone involved is willing to cooperate with each other. It is a game of give and take. You must understand that in order to help yourself, you must help others. The only obstacle standing between you and any goal you should desire to achieve is the cooperation and support of those around you. Your so-called "piece of the pie" will be in direct proportion to the size of your circle of friends.

"If you desire the help of others, help others first."

When you help lift others to success through your cooperative nature, you will soon discover an outreached arm ready to pull you up as well. Make every effort possible to help fill the needs of others, and you will discover that your needs, too, are met, because it is not possible to hold a light for another without having your own path lit. If you desire the help of others, help others first. When you invest your time and energy in helping others, it always pays high dividends. To win a friend, do someone a favor.

The only hope for betterment of the world is through learning to cooperate and be unified in our desire to improve our current conditions. Until we realize that our world will not improve unless the world of others is improved, we are fighting a hopeless battle. Luke 11:17B says, *"Any kingdom divided against itself will be ruined, and a house divided against itself will fall."* When we are willing to cooperate with others, they will be our allies. Our peace with our self, and with the rest of the world, is dependent on our ability to cooperate with those we meet. Success begets success; working together enables all to prosper.

Teamwork enables us to *divide* the effort and *multiply* the results, as well as *add* to our list of friends. Understand that cooperation does not always mean that each party will carry equal shares of the load, but it does mean working together and doing what you can. A team does not consist of a certain number of individuals; it is a whole, with unified parts. Two working together will many times produce more than ten working alone. When we realize that we are "all in this together," and decide to unify our efforts through cooperation, the sky is the limit in regards to what can be achieved. Cooperation increases productivity, and if we can put our differences in the back seat, and pay attention to where we are going, we will get there sooner and saner.

"We need to learn how to tear down walls and use the material from them to build bridges."

Until you realize that you were created to help others, and others were created to help you, you will not feel the need to cooperate. For how beneficial are we to the world if we only look out for ourselves? Believe it or not, the world is larger than just what you can see. We need to learn how to tear down walls and use the material from them to build bridges. The power of the river is due to the cooperation of the individual raindrops.

Henry Ford said, *"Coming together is a beginning; staying together is progress; working together is success."* If we do unto others what we would have them do unto us, our world would be one of joy and success.

There is no such thing as a "self-made" person. First of all, God donated by far the largest contribution; others next to the biggest, and self barely gave at all. In regards to life, if you are not equipped to lead, and are unwilling to follow, then do everyone a favor and stay home! However, if you have a spirit of cooperation and are looking for a full life, the next time someone asks, "Have you ever slain a dragon?" Just smile and say, *"Nope, but I have always wanted to!"*

*****

"So in everything, do to others what you would have them do to you, for this sums up the Law and the Prophets." [Matthew 7:12]

10 - Buckle Up, Boys, We're Going In!

I am not sure where I first heard the order, *"Buckle up, boys, we're going in,"* but I do remember where I have heard it the most in recent years. It was a favorite saying of one of our past shepherds at church. Every time we had an issue or problem, John would get this sheepish grin on his face and say, *"Buckle up, boys, we're going in!"* We knew that meant we were in for some excitement, and that we needed to drag out our "coats of courage" because things were about to change.

"Obstacles are overcome first in the head and then in the heart."

The more I think about it, the more I believe that *"Buckle up, boys, we're going in,"* would be a good motto for us as we prepare for each day of our lives. As we all know, it takes courage to face some of the daily issues that we will encounter. And with an attitude that goes along with this motto, the world would know we mean business. For the best way to confront difficulties is head-on, and with courage.

Courage is defined as the power to face difficulties, and it comes from a special reserve of the mind that is more powerful than outside circumstances. We must be bigger than, or equal to, our problems, and it is through courage that we are able to do just that. Obstacles are overcome first in the head and then in the heart. When the battle is won in your mind, the odds go up tremendously in your favor.

Columnist Ann Landers once remarked, *"If I were asked to give what I consider the single most useful bit of advice for all humanity, it would be this: Expect trouble as an inevitable part of life and when it comes, hold your head high, look it in the eye and say, 'I will be bigger than you. You can't defeat me."*

Instilled within each individual is a reserve of courage that enables us to look life in the face and ask, "You want a piece of this?" Courage and perseverance cause difficulties to do a disappearing act. Courage is the will to live put into action. For the best-made plans are useless unless someone has the courage to put them into action. Discouragement dwells in the den of despair; courage cleans house!

We must be careful not to allow our thoughts to control our actions (or lack of), for sometimes, our thoughts are incorrect. I remember a story about the late magician / daredevil Harry Houdini, and how he would challenge anyone to construct a jail cell that he could not break out of in a matter of minutes. The only requirements were that he be allowed to go in, dressed in his street clothes, without an audience, as he prepared his "jail break." If my memory serves correctly, the one particular jail that accepted the challenge was in the Bahamas. Houdini worked feverishly with the tools he had smuggled in, but to no avail. Minutes passed, then hours. Finally, Houdini gave up, exhausted, and fell against the door, which opened without resistance. You see, the door had never been locked, except in the mind of Houdini! Sometimes we, too, remain locked behind bars that are only locked in our minds. When we believe the lock has been set, we give up hope and therefore never bother calling on our courage to take charge. With courage as the backbone, a person can stand straight and face the opponent in battle.

> ***"With courage as the backbone, a person can stand straight and face the opponent in battle."***

Andrew Jackson said, *"One man with courage makes a majority."* To face opposition with enough courage to take a stand, even if you lose the battle, you win a war! Courage must be laced with an understanding that even if you lose, you win because you did not back down.

I have heard fear defined as "**F**alse **E**vidence **A**ppearing **R**eal." There is much truth to this statement, as many times we believe something to be true, even though falsehood surrounds it. The problem is that if we believe it to be true, we will approach it as if it were true. Our minds are a marvelous piece of equipment, and can be our greatest friend or our fiercest foe.

Jerome P. Fleishman said, *"It takes courage to live - courage and strength and hope and humor. And courage and strength and hope and humor have to be bought and paid for with pain and work and prayers and tears."*

Yes, the price of living life with courage will cost us, but it is well worth it. For to give up in the face of resistance is to lose hope, and eventually give into whatever it is we are facing. You can overcome whatever obstacles you face if you have courage, strength, hope and humor.

You know what I am going to tell you, don't you? *"Buckle up, boys, we're going in!"*

*****

"Have I not commanded you? Be strong and courageous. Do not be terrified; do not be discouraged, for the Lord your God will be with you wherever you go." [Joshua 1:9]

11 - Antidisestablishmentarianism

There are few things I remember from sixth grade, but the word *"antidisestablishmentarianism"* (it was at the time the longest word in the English language) is one I do. This was a "bonus" word on a spelling test. I can still remember how to spell it, and I can still remember the meaning of it: "Do not tear down what has been built up!" Now I will be the first to admit that it is difficult to use the word antidisestablishmentarianism in normal conversation, but the meaning of it is good advice for any of us, unless, of course, you are in the demolition business. Even then, it is good advice to heed when you deal with people. I have heard that it takes ten positive comments to overcome the harm done by only one negative comment, so we need to make sure we are not in the habit of being negative and critical in our dealings with others. Why don't we all adopt the word *"antidisestablishmentarianism"* and its meaning as our motto to live by? The world would be a much better place to live.

It is a fact that if you attempt to do anything, you are opening the door for critics - but do not allow that to stop you. Just remember that it is much easier to be a critic than a contestant. However, it is wise to listen to the words of critics for possible ways to improve, but do not allow them to steal your hopes and dreams. Words of criticism can be beneficial if they are true, and if they are delivered with the right motive. If a mistake is pointed out in the work of another, it can be of great help in allowing them an opportunity for improving.

An Arabian proverb goes like this, *"If one person calls you an ass or a donkey, pay no attention to him. But if five people call you one, go out and buy yourself a saddle."* If the criticism we receive is true, then we need to make every possible effort to correct our error. If it is false, we need to forget about it and go on with life. Each of us must keep our ears open and our mouth shut when being criticized because there may be a valuable lesson being taught. When we receive criticism and become a better person for it, we should consider it a valuable gift.

Everyone produces more and better work under the supervision of approval than under a critical eye. For you see, it is easy to be critical, but being factual comes a bit harder. If you are not doing anything, people will criticize you for being lazy. If you are daring enough to do something, people will criticize you for not doing it right. Err on the side of doing something instead of nothing!

Before we allow criticism to escape from our lips, we should make every effort to try and understand exactly where the other person is coming from, and why they act/react the way they do. We often criticize what we don't understand, and, therefore, our words can cause tremendous damage to the one at which they are directed.

It takes no special talent to get set up in the "fault finding business." However, some people act as if there is a reward for finding fault, and they search them out as treasure. The funny thing about it is that most people have a knack for finding the faults in others and overlooking their own. My feeling is that unless we are willing to enter the ring ourselves, we have no right to criticize the boxer or even the referee.

"It takes no special talent to set up in the fault-finding business."

I believe the words of Abraham Lincoln are worth repeating in the area of criticism. *"If I were to read, much less answer, all the attacks made on me, this shop might as well be closed for any other business. I do the very best I know how - the very best I can, and I mean to keep doing so until the end. If the end brings me out all right, what is said against me won't amount to anything. If the end brings me out wrong, ten angels swearing I was right would make no difference."*

It is impossible to find any performance that pleases everyone in every way. It is easy to find fault in others, and difficult to personally present a more perfect plan. Only the speakers who never spoke are found to be without fault. If you wait until you are assured you can do something so well that no one will criticize you, you are not going to accomplish much. It is a fact that we are all different in some ways. However, we need to be careful in pointing out the shortcomings of others, for our own deficiencies may stand tall by comparison. To hold your tongue and temper in the face of criticism will be more of a testimony to your integrity than anything you could say in defense.

I like the way Tyne Daly defined a critic when he said, *"A critic is someone who never actually goes to the battle yet who afterwards comes out shooting the wounded."* If we really stop and think about it, that is what happens in many cases of criticism. It is much easier to sit in the stands, or in our easy chair, and bad-mouth the quality of play or refereeing, than it is to be on the field and a part of the battle. Before you criticize, understand that whatever you say about someone will probably get back to them, so if you are not willing to say it to their face, don't say it behind their back.

In all your dealings with others, I still believe the best policy is just "*antidisestablishmentarianism.*" And if you should find it difficult to fit it into your conversation, that is OK. Just fit it into your life.

*****

>   "*Always be prepared to give an answer to everyone who asks you to give the reason for the hope that you have. But do this with gentleness and respect.*"
>   [1 Peter 3:15b-17]

12 - Courage Is Found In Encouragement

If the number of encouragements a person receives has anything to do with the level of blessings in a life, then I have lived a blessed life. I can think of encounters of encouragement too numerous to mention all through my life.

For those of you who know me personally, you may have a hard time believing that I was a very shy and withdrawn person all through my high school years. However, I have been able to overcome most of the poor self-image I had of myself through the help of many people, but most of all, because of my wife, Linda. She has been, and continues to be, a never-ending source of encouragement to me. Linda and other members of my family, plus numerous friends, have helped me tremendously with their words of encouragement. Just this past week, I celebrated my 60th birthday, and I cannot begin to tell you how much positive feedback I was offered. In addition, just today, I received a very uplifting note from my friend Andy, who encouraged me by saying that I had been an encouragement to him.

I am here to tell you, *"Courage is found in encouragement."* Each of us has a responsibility to allow ourselves to be used as an instrument of encouragement to others.

We must never underestimate the impact that a simple act of kindness can have in the life of someone else. If you will take the time to encourage others, you will be encouraged yourself. May we all be at "Home On The Range" by holding to the rule, *"Where never is heard a discouraging word, and the skies are not cloudy all day."* For words of encouragement, do have a way of lifting clouds out of people's days and helping them have hope. HOPE has been said to stand for *"Hanging On, Praying Expectantly."* Trust and confidence in another will offer them the hope to continue, when the world tries to get them to give up.

"Every person has the need to be needed and appreciated."

Every person needs to be needed and appreciated. If each of us would only take part in doing "random acts of encouragement," as we have been encouraged to do random acts of kindness, oh, what a difference we could make in this world! Words of encouragement are medicine for a disheartened heart. Dare yourself to catch someone doing well, and encourage him or her. This will empower them to do even better. A life without encouragement is a certain, slow death.

Productivity is hindered by lack of encouragement. Many businesses across our country never realize their true potential because they do not offer an environment of encouragement. By finding the good in others and pointing it out, we make them better still. It has been said that you can draw more bees with honey (kind words) than you can with vinegar (sour words). We need to look for the good in others with the same intensity that gold miners look for gold. If we do this, we will help fill them with self-worth and enable them to do their best. Here are three, three-letter words to offer encouragement: *"Yes you can!"*

"A life without encouragement is a certain, slow death."

There is no way to measure the good that can come from the impact of even one word of encouragement. If you think someone is deserving of praise, please pass it on. However, if you think someone is deserving of degrading words, please do everyone a favor and keep them to yourself! Let your imagination run wild with ways to encourage others, but keep it in solitary confinement when tempted to discourage.

My advice is to believe in others even before they believe in themselves, for in so doing, you may be the turning point their life. It happens all the time. Few, if any, ever founder on words of encouragement.

One of the most rewarding feelings in the world is to know you have helped another succeed by your words and acts of encouragement. Words of approval lead to works of acclaim; critical comments lead to crummy conditions. Nit-picking is a no-no if you wish to be helpful in building up another. However, to feel appreciated is as vital a need to the soul as air is to the body. People will have a tendency to try harder if they believe you believe in them. Not only in the Third World countries, but all over the world, people are starving for words of encouragement.

Your words hold within them the power to give life or death to those you meet, so be very careful in how you use them. People will strive to live up to words of praise, and be better than they would have without them. On the other hand, words of discouragement can kill any hope that may have been present and might prevent someone from even attempting to do anything.

"Encouragement is a powerful and necessary tool in everyone's life."

Encouragement is a powerful and necessary tool in everyone's life. It is often said to be the most powerful tool known for lifting a person above their own expectations, and allowing them to be all they can be. Encouragement is the energy needed to keep running when you feel like calling it quits. There is one sure way to tell if a person needs encouragement - if they are still breathing, they need it!

It has been said that it takes nine encouraging comments to overcome the negative impact of one critical comment. Therefore, we need to be extra careful as parents to make sure the words we feed our children are those of encouragement, and not those that make them second-guess their worth as a person. Remember, *"Courage is found in encouragement!"*

*****

"Therefore encourage one another and build each other up, just as in fact you are doing." [1 Thessalonians 5:11]

13 - Rich, But Bankrupt

Have you ever known anyone who possessed all the good things of this life and yet in the real sense was worse off than any bankrupt individual? I believe that description befits anyone who has lost his or her enthusiasm for life. H. W. Arnold once said, *"The worst bankrupt in the world is the man that has lost his enthusiasm."* It does not matter how uneducated or simple you might be, if you have enthusiasm you will find yourself more powerful and influential than the wisest person who is plagued with complacency.

Enthusiasm is not an automatic response in everyday adult life. It must be fed and nourished by attempting new things and thinking new thoughts. If you noticed I stated in *adult life*, as you do not have to look far to find the enthusiasm in youth. The question is, "What happens to it?" It is a fact that some people's spirits grow gray before their hair. However, most people grow old, not from playing but because they quit playing. None are so old as those who have outlived their enthusiasm for life. Samuel Ullman wrote, *"To give up enthusiasm wrinkles the soul."* The truth is that adulthood will knock enthusiasm to its knees if we let it. It can knock the wind out of us. But few things carry a more powerful punch in the ring of life than enthusiasm. With enthusiasm in your corner, the opponent has little chance of winning.

> *"With enthusiasm in your corner, the opponent has little chance of winning."*

The word enthusiasm comes from the word "entheous" meaning "God within." In the real world, God never leaves us, but the worries of the world will certainly overshadow his presence and control our lives if we are not careful. One warning in regard to enthusiasm - make sure we are only competing with ourselves, and trying to break our own personal best, not out-doing someone else. One of the quickest and surest ways to become discouraged is to compare our accomplishments with those who possess talents completely different from ours.

The person who partners with enthusiasm and joins forces with gratitude cannot help but be blessed in his fight against the pitfalls of everyday living. If you are not willing to tackle any project with enthusiasm, then at least sit in the stands and cheer for the one who is. Most any battle can be won when enthusiasm is your ammo of choice, for no matter the enemy, all will eventually fall and the war will be won. The degree of your fever of enthusiasm will determine how sick your opponent will feel.

No matter how many years we have lived, our choice of words will speak volumes in the regard to our level of maturity. Enthusiasm punctuates our life and insists that we use exclamation marks instead of periods. If your wish is to excel in any avenue of life, apply an extra measure of effort peppered with enthusiasm and watch the results.

"Enthusiasm is the nourishment that keeps progress alive."

Enthusiasm is the nourishment that keeps progress alive. With it, higher bars will be jumped. Without it, we will be flat on our backs, looking up. When we find ourselves down and depressed, finding something to be enthusiastic about will help us to our knees and then standing tall. Let it be said, if I am to be found guilty, I wish it to be on the side of enthusiasm and suffering defeat, than to be indifferent and wearing the garland of victory.

Let's face it - we are going to do foolish things from time to time, but if we can remember to do them with enthusiasm, we will be more ready to laugh with others than to cry by ourselves. And, remember, enthusiasm is much better bait for catching recruits than any "threat net" ever will be. So how about it, are you ready to make a withdrawal from your enthusiasm bank, or are you already bankrupt?

*****

"Never be lacking in zeal, but keep your spiritual fervor, serving the Lord." [Romans 12:11]

14 - Excuse Me For My Excuse!

I have used every excuse I could think of to convince myself not to write on the subject of excuses, but none of them were convincing enough, so here goes.

When we talk about the excuses that students use for a reason why they do not have their homework done on time, the one that comes to mind first is, "The dog ate it." It just so happened that this is exactly what Jimmy told Mr. Stewart when asked why he didn't have his work completed. However, Mr. Stewart wasn't buying it for one minute. However, Jimmy insisted that it was true. He finally admitted, "He didn't want to, but I made him!"

That is sort of where I am on this subject; I didn't want to write about it, but my conscience made me! Would you be so kind as to *"Excuse me for my excuse!"*?

Very few people are skillful (or should I say "deceitful") enough to make an excuse sound good enough to pass for the truth. It has been determined that an excuse is a close relative to a lie. However, when I talk about my own, "excuse" is much easier to accept than "lie" is. So if you don't mind, I will reserve "lie" for when I am referring to **your** excuses.

When a person doesn't want to do something, an excuse is their way out of it. And in a situation like this, it really doesn't matter if it even sounds real or not, because one excuse is as good as another when you have already made up your mind. Losers will use circumstances as excuses, while winners will make the most of what they have. A person who always has an excuse has very little to show for the work he didn't do. I have always heard, *"Excuses are a dime a dozen,"* but I have to tell you that I wouldn't even give you that much for them. And the truth of the matter is that others won't either. People do not want excuses, they want results.

Having an interest in and a love for something will find a way to do it, while an attitude of indifference will make excuses. An excuse is simply a crutch for the liar. Once a person decides to accept responsibility for his or her mistakes, excuses are of no need. Pointing the finger of blame at someone else is the "granddaddy" of all excuses (reference Genesis chapter 3).

> *"Once a person decides to accept responsibility for their mistakes, excuses are of no need."*

It seems that one day last winter, an employee with the census bureau was forty-five minutes late getting to work. He was explaining his tardiness to the boss and said, *"It was so slippery out that for every step I tried to take ahead, I slipped back two."* The boss was a bit suspicious. *"Oh yeah? Then how did you ever manage to get here?"* The clever fellow explained, *"I finally just gave up, and started for home."* (I hate to admit it, but it makes sense to me.)

In any area of life, success does not come to the one who stays busy making excuses. If we cannot find a way to accomplish something, rather than make an excuse, we need to get busy and make a way. Excuses are seldom found in the camp of the ambitious. A capable builder will not blame his saw for a crooked cut.

To set yourself up for failure, start making excuses early, and you will find failure soon enough. A success built on the foundation of excuses will not stand for long. A cup of performance is worth more than a boatload of excuses.

Some mess up their mess-ups by making excuses, rather than fess us! (Wow! Try saying that ten times real fast without messing up.) Excuses rarely satisfy anyone except their owner. A good rule to follow is, if you would not accept an excuse as a legitimate reason, then do not attempt to use it on someone else. Actually, a better rule to follow would be to not use excuses at all. Just admit to your mistake and move on. A loser is a person that makes excuses for their behavior and will not accept responsibility.

Making an excuse for a mistake actually doubles the mistake. We need to understand, the more excuses a person offers, the less truth there is to any of them. An excuse is simply a way of covering up something that one would rather not admit. Accepting the responsibility for a mistake is a sign of character.

Little Johnny was visiting his grandmother one summer at her home in Louisiana. Granny asked him to take her bucket, go down to the river, and bring back some water to wash clothes with. When little Johnny got to the river, he was frightened by two eyes staring back at him, so he dropped the bucket and ran for the house. When he got back, Granny asked, *"Where is my bucket of water?"* Johnny told her, *"There is an alligator down there, and I got scared and left it at the river."* Granny assured him, *"That alligator has been down there for years and has never caused anyone any harm. As a matter of fact, that* alligator is probably just as scared of you as you are of him." Johnny's reply was, *"If that's the case, that water ain't fit to wash clothes in no-how!"* Now I am not sure if you would consider Johnny's explanation an excuse or not, but I must admit that I am on his side.

> **"An excuse is simply a way of covering up something that one would rather not admit."**

All of us are in the manufacturing business; some of us make good, some make bad, and some make excuses. And I am sorry to say that even a few of us are good at making bad excuses. If I should happen to fall into this last category, I just want to say, *"It's not my fault!"* Oh, well, on second thought, maybe it is. So, if you don't mind, *"Excuse me for my excuse."*

*****

Jesus replied: "A certain man was preparing a great banquet and inviting many guests. At the time of the banquet he sent his servant to tell those who had been invited, 'Come, for everything is now ready.' But they all alike began to make excuses. The first one said, 'I have just bought a field, and I must go and see it. Please excuse me.' Another said, 'I have just bought five yoke of oxen, and I'm on my way to try them out. Please excuse me.' Still another said, 'I just got married, so I can't come.' The servant came back and reported this to his master. Then the owner of the house became angry and ordered his servant, go out quickly into the streets and alleys of the town and bring in the poor, the crippled, the

blind and the lame. 'Sir', the servant said, 'what you ordered has been done, but there is still room.' Then the master told his servant, 'Go out to the roads and country lanes and make them come in, so that my house will be full. I tell you, not one of those men who were invited will get a taste of my banquet."
[Luke 14:16-24]

15 - Down, But Not Out

.:.~

I have watched boxing matches where the fighter I had picked to win is knocked to the mat. However, I have never witnessed anyone who stayed down win the fight. For you see, it doesn't matter how many times you fall as long as the number of times you get up is one greater. The same is true in our lives; we will be knocked down occasionally, but as long as we do not stay there, the victory **can** be ours. So the next time you get knocked to the mat in your bout with life, lift your head and tell yourself that you may be *down, but not out*. Get to your feet and finish the good fight.

Our minds have a tendency to speak "negativism" as its natural tongue. We must take the initiative to learn the positive language of love and speak it everywhere we go. If those listening happen not to understand, then accept the role as mentor and get started teaching.

We have a tendency to use every excuse imaginable before looking inwardly to find the real fault. However, when we do find it and make the necessary corrections, progress will have been made both outwardly and inwardly. If we do not learn from our mistakes, we will remain uneducated in regard to our full potential.

A man can fail many times, but when he lays the blame on someone else, he shall be crowned the "King of Fools." The only true failure is the one who has adopted blame as a member of the family. Pride keeps us from saying, "I was wrong," but when we force ourselves to voice those words, bridges can be built. When you prepare a place to sleep and leave room for blame to lie alongside, do not be surprised to find failure as your bedfellow.

"Failing is not truly failing until it is replaced by idleness."

It seems ironic, I admit, but success is what causes many people to become failures. The easiest and most natural thing to do after succeeding is to be blinded by all the glory and never notice the needs of those around you. The achievement of a goal should never be our final destination, but a station of rest on our journey of life.

Failing is not truly failing until it is replaced by idleness. I think you will find it true that most failures usually hike the path of least resistance. We must be constantly aware and never allow the fear from past failures to prevent us from preparing for the future. To lose interest in finishing a task is not fatal; however, never rekindling the fire will be.

When we understand that mistakes are a sure sign of something happening it is much easier to accept them. If we accept failure as being final, we will drop out and never receive a degree in accomplishment. In fighting the battle against disappointment, we will be enlightened to know that victory lies just over the next hill.

We can fail just as surely from attempting too much as we can from attempting too little. Many times the busyness of trying to succeed will cause us to take our eyes off what is most important. A sure-fire guarantee for failure is to try to make **all** others happy.

One who gives less than their best in any situation could rightly be tagged a failure. We must not become discouraged by making the mistake of comparing our accomplishments with others'. As long as we have done everything to the best of our ability, we have the right to declare ourselves a winner.

"Failing is not fatal unless it prevents us from trying again."

Failure is not fatal unless it prevents us from trying again. However, we need to make sure that every attempt made after a defeat is evident of a bit more wisdom. Logic tells us that if we can learn from our mistakes, we should make more of them. Just do not allow re-runs! Pencils come with more lead than eraser for a reason. On average, when the eraser is gone, you should be writing with little more than a nub. If most of the lead is still present when the eraser has vanished, you may wish to seek counsel.

*****

"Love never fails." 1 Corinthians 13:8a

16 - That Scared Me, And I Ain't Scared Of Nothing!

I use the phrase, *"That scared me, and I ain't scared of nothing!"* a lot, but I will have to admit that it is not the whole truth. For I am not that much different (I said "that much") from anyone else. We all have things that come in the form of fear that cripple our creative juices; it is our duty to get a handle on them and not allow them to paralyze us. I do not know what it is that you are afraid of; maybe it is the dark, maybe it is a disease, maybe it is your job situation, maybe it is your family or someone close to you. It does not matter what it is because you can learn to control it and rule it, rather than let it be master over you. I can assure you of one thing: if it weren't for the fear of being called a coward, more people would give in to admitting that they, too, are afraid. I tell you that it is OK to be afraid sometimes - just don't let it own you!

I have found that fear is usually the result of not knowing all the facts, and allowing our imagination to determine what is real and what is not. Fear doesn't have a leg to stand on when we gather the facts and are certain of surrounding circumstances. For fear, playing with our imagination, can make our fears seem larger than life itself. Fear will play "mind games" with you and laugh at you when it wins. Unfortunately, to entertain your fears is no fun at all.

"Nothing renders the mind powerless like fear does."

John Lennon made this comment; *"The unknown is what it is. And to be frightened of it is what sends everybody scurrying around chasing dreams, illusions, war, peace, love, hate, and all that. Unknown is what it is. Accept that it's unknown, and it's plain sailing."* If we can get a grip on the truth that what scares us most is that which remains unknown to us, we have a great chance to overcome. Nothing renders the mind powerless like fear. However, do the thing that scares you most, and soon you will be filled with hope, and actually looking forward to the challenge.

A person filled with fear and doubt has no need for any other enemies to overcome him - he is already a prisoner of war! Fear is an emotion and can only have the power we entrust to it. If we decide to take that power away, it will melt and eventually evaporate. But to relinquish the thoughts of the mind to fear is to name fear as lord of lords. Courage, however, can put fear in its rightful place. It is true that when fear takes up residence in our minds, it is hard to get it evicted. But it can be done! Fear is a powerful force and can only be tamed by faith, and the courage to take action.

Funny, but fear can make one freeze in their tracks and sweat profusely at the same time. Fear prevents more good from being accomplished than any other circumstance. It robs the mind of its power to think straight. Babe Ruth once said, *"Never let the fear of striking out get in your way."*

Fear is the number one enemy in preventing a person from enjoying life. Fear is engaged in war with your thoughts, and will take the heart as its prisoner. When we can find the courage to face our fears, the battle is mostly won. When fear is faced with action, it loses!

"Fear can consume a person's thoughts and paralyze them from attempting to live."

Fear is a fire that will either warm you when kept under control, or destroy you when it gets out of hand. It has a way of making us believe that the worst will happen. We need to realize that even if it does, it is not the end of the world. Fear can consume a person's thoughts and paralyze them from attempting to live. Actually, the thing in life that scares most people is life itself. When fear fills the mind, you can give up the hope of having any sane thoughts. If you ever want to make a person useless, instill fear in them.

Fear, worry and doubt will wear you out physically, mentally and spiritually. If we allow our fears to exist, they will eventually steal the will to live. Fear that is permitted to grow will overcome the mind in which it resides, and its favorite food is uncertainty.

It is funny how the same level of fear that makes you cautious makes the other person a coward. All carry fear with them into battle, but some allow fear to become the commander and end up as cowards. It is fact that a person who tells you that he has never been scared will lie to you about other things as well.

Franklin D. Roosevelt's famous quote about fear goes like this: *"The only thing we have to fear is fear itself - nameless, unreasoning, unjustified terror which paralyzes needed efforts to convert retreat into advance."* Many times fear is nameless, but at other times we are very familiar with its name and some even go as far as adopting it as a permanent member of the family. It is always unreasoning and unjustified, and it will prevent us from having the courage to face what lies ahead. Moreover, courage is nothing more than the result of putting our fears to bed.

Fear is a sure sign of mind over matter, and will not permit hope to visit. What, no hope? *"Now that scared me, and I ain't scared of nothing!"*

*****

"God is our refuge and strength, an ever-present help in trouble. Therefore we will not fear, though the earth give way and the mountains fall into the heart of the sea, though its waters roar and foam and the mountains quake with their surging." [Psalm 46:1-3]

17 - I forgive you....but!

A number of years ago an exchange student lived with us for a year while she went to school in our country. One of the things I remember most is something she told us that neither Linda nor I could comprehend. She shared the fact even though she and her sister shared the same bedroom, there had been a period of almost three years when they had not spoken to one another. That fact alone was hard enough to believe, but the one that made it totally unbelievable was that when I asked her what they had been mad about, she could not remember! How in the world could two people waste three precious years of their lives and not remember what caused the conflict to start with? Another sad part is that I know this is not an isolated incident. The sin of not forgiving is a thief in the truest sense of the word. I am happy to be able to report in the case of our former exchange student and her sister, they are now "best friends." Oh, if every story could end in such a happy way.

We need to be in the business of forgetting the wrongs that have been committed to us, and remembering the ones we have committed against others, not for "self-incrimination," but for the purpose of not making them again. Forgiveness must start in the heart of the one who has been wronged. However, it must proceed forth from there and make a landing in the heart of the one being forgiven. If they refuse to accept your act of love and peace, go on about your life, knowing you did what you should have.

"Forgiveness must start in the heart of the one who has been wronged."

I am not sure who to credit with the following quote, as I found both Thomas Fuller and Lord Herbert listed under it in different publications. Nevertheless, I believe it worth repeating. It says, *"He that cannot forgive others, breaks the bridge over which he must pass himself; for every man has need to be forgiven."* Can I hear an "Amen?" [Oops. Forgive me, please. For I really feel that if I have to ask for an "amen," I could be the only one who believes it is deserved.] To have been hurt and never forgive the offender is to be hurt afresh every day!

Seems odd, but most people have no trouble remembering all the times they have forgiven others. So much for the "forgive and forget" duo.

The open wound caused by being wronged will never completely heal until we allow the "salve of forgiveness" to be applied. It takes a strong person to forgive a hurt and a weak person to relive one. To carry a grudge is too heavy a load for anyone.

Please, for your sake, grant forgiveness to all who have offended you. In doing so, you will receive the greater gifts of peace and happiness. Carrying the load of not forgiving will cause your spirit to die from "self-inflicted" wounds. To be unwilling to forgive the faults of others will be a fault far heavier of your own. We must be willing to let go of the desire to return hurt, in retaliation for injuries we may have incurred. It is a fact that a person who will not take the steps to forgive will certainly have a short list of friends. Few lessons are so hard to learn as forgiveness, fewer still offer such soft rewards.

"To carry a grudge is too heavy a load for anyone."

Henry Ward Beecher once said, *"I can forgive, but I cannot forget is only another way of saying, I will not forgive. Forgiveness ought to be like a cancelled note - torn in two and burned up so that it never can be shown against one."* Forgiveness means "letting go and letting God." It does not mean that you will never recall the incident again, but it does mean that you are willing to relinquish the desire for revenge.

Sometimes it is easier to forgive others than to forgive yourself. So allow me to allow you to be selfish just this once; even if the offender shows no signs of accepting your acts of forgiveness, be selfish and forgive yourself! For sad indeed is the one who cannot forgive him or herself.

"Sometimes it is easier to forgive others than it is to forgive ourselves."

Dwight L. Moody said, *"I firmly believe a great many prayers are not answered because we are unwilling to forgive someone."* If you have been wondering why you haven't heard anything back in answer to some of your pleas, this could be the reason.

If you ever hear someone say, *"I forgive you...but,"* you know they truly have not and are just saying the first part to console themselves. However, go ahead and be the more mature person - forgive them, even if their but is in the way!

*****

> *"For if you forgive men when they sin against you, your heavenly Father will also forgive you. But if you do not forgive men their sins, your Father will not forgive your sins."* [Matthew 6:14-15]

18 - Bosom Buddies

I remember reading a story a number of years ago where a soldier from WWI asked permission from his commanding officer to go after his wounded friend who still lay in harm's way. The officer advised the young GI against it, but allowed him to make the final choice. The young man knew he was risking his life if he helped his wounded friend. But he knew the decision he had to make —- it would have been the same decision his friend would have made had the circumstances been reversed. He managed to get to his wounded friend and hoist him onto his shoulders for travel back to the trenches. Both men tumbled into the foxhole at the same time. The officer surveyed the situation and was quick to say, "I told you it wouldn't be worth it. Your friend is dead and you are mortally wounded!" To which the young soldier replied, "Oh but it was worth it, sir. For my friend was still alive when I got to him and he said 'I knew you would come after me, Mike. So to me, it was more than worth it, sir."

If you have been blessed to have had a friend like this G.I., you know just how great a gift friendship is. If you have not experienced it yet, I hope and pray you will. My life has been blessed in this area on more than one occasion, but the one that has had the greatest impact was my brother-in-law, Gary. He and I either visited or talked with each other nearly every day, and we felt comfortable in sharing our hearts with one another. We both knew that if one of us had a need, the other would be there to fill it.

I will never forget the day in 1998 when I received a phone call telling me that Gary had been killed in a motorcycle accident. I was in Missouri for a sales meeting at the time, otherwise I am sure I would have been riding with him. I think the Lord knew that I would not have been able to cope had I witnessed the accident, so He made sure I was out of town. The redeye flight back home that night was one of the longest I have ever experienced. The hole is still there, but time is a marvelous healer. Through the past 10 years I have been blessed with other friends who, I truly believe, would go so far as to lay down their life for me if the need arose. However, losing even one friend in a lifetime is one too many. If our life is stripped of a true friend through distance or death, a void will occur that cannot be filled. Our only hope is for another friend.

If we can come to the understanding that we are not that good, and others are not that bad, there is no reason why a friendship cannot flourish. One of the greatest gifts we will ever unwrap is that of getting to know a friend and allowing time to make that friendship a most prized possession that we can continue to unwrap daily. If we are to call each other "friend," then we must be willing to defend each other's reputation, stand in the gap for, be open and honest with, and remain true to each other even when the world calls us "fool."

"True friendship is never one-sided."

A true friend will be an ocean of openness, a sea of sincerity and a river of reasons to live. Nothing offers such comfort as a friend who feels your ache. Friendship should always be a salve for the sores of life, never the cause of the pain. In the end, the hearts we have touched, and the hearts we have allowed to touch ours will measure the value of our life. Just as an eagle needs a nest and a spider needs a web, a man needs the warmth of a friendship from which he draws comfort.

Each party in a friendship must accept responsibility to make it work. True friendship is never one-sided. Time spent with a friend is not wasted - unproductive maybe with few noticeable results, but it is never wasted. The prescription that always produces positive results against our temporal ills is a good dose of friendship.

Few things bring a good night's rest on a cold winter's night faster than your favorite pillow, a warm blanket and the thought of a friend who has tucked you into the folds of their heart.

I cannot remember where I first heard or read it, but a quote that has been with me since that day says, *"Each man should keep within himself a small cemetery in which to bury the faults of his friends."* For a life with no friends would be like a slow death. In order to keep the doors of friendship open, we must close our eyes and ears to the faults of others. Praise the qualities of your friends and they will flock to be by your side; belittle them and they flee.

"Life is much more enjoyable when shared with another."

It is near impossible to live a life of contentment without the favor of friends. Want to see a portrait of God? Look no farther than the face of a friend.

As we travel the road of life, will our souvenirs be mere trinkets or treasures of friendships? Life is much more enjoyable when shared with another. If a person has a lot of friends, it is a pretty good bet that one of two things is the reason; either he has a big bank account or he takes the time to listen when others talk. Hey, don't stick your hand out to me - I'm listening!

*****

"My command is this: Love each other as I have loved you. Greater love has no one than this, that he lay down his life for his friends. You are my friends if you do what I command." [John 15:12-14]

19 - Oh, Give Me A Break!

Let's admit it, sometimes life happens and we just feel like saying, *"Oh, give me a break!"* Now this could be in almost any area of life, depending on the situation at hand. However, I believe we need to direct our focus on ourselves and realize that if we want others to give us a break, we must be willing to give them one first. The laws of nature tell us that we will receive in proportion to what we have given. The principle is the same everywhere and in every aspect of our lives. You cannot get over it, under it, around it or through it. You must give to receive, and, what you give will be the bounty of what you sow. A Chinese Proverb goes like this: *"Sow much, reap much. Sow little, reap little."* That pretty well sums it up when it comes to the principles involved in the art of giving as well as the art of living.

If you want to bless your life, bless the lives of others. It is nothing more than the generosity of the heart that will determine the generosity of the gifts the heart receives. Those who wish to be known as the "go-getters" in life need to realize that first they must be known as the "go-givers." What you keep for yourself is temporary; what you give away will last forever. We could search the world over for an example of when one gave away without getting anything in return, and our search would be fruitless.

"If you want to bless your life, bless the lives of others."

As we walk through life each day, we should always be looking for a place to sow a few seeds of joy and kindness. In future walks along the same paths, we will notice the brilliant colors of the flowers of love and peace that have grown. Then we will be able to adorn our tables with bouquets of both. Let's not be stingy in sowing the seeds of the fruit we would most like to enjoy.

We should count it a blessing the day we are able to give and not remember, and receive but not forget! For of all virtues, giving is the greatest! We should strive to add value to whatever gift we give by doing so joyfully.

Every man should make it his business to benefit and bless others. When it is, his business will boom. When our business is our business, it will bust. To reap much, serve much! We should do our best to surprise others by giving them more than they expect, and, in turn, we, too, will be surprised when we receive more than we expected.

Andrew Cordier once remarked, *"It should be our purpose in life to see that each of us makes a contribution as will enable us to say that we, individually and collectively, are a part of the answer to the world problem and not a part of the problem itself."* If you have trouble with the answer to that issue, I would dare say you do have a problem.

If we expect others to be generous, we need to make sure we are setting the type of example they most need to see. We should never feel shame in the size of the gift we have to offer, for to the receiver it may mean more than we can imagine. Those who are willing to share in the small things are generally willing to share in the larger ones as well. The greatest part of the gift is many times the love in which it is wrapped.

Our hearts are open to give when we take our eyes off ourselves and look to the needs of others. For one to say he would give more if he had more and yet is unwilling to share what he has, is, among other things, a liar. Each of us should be ashamed, if at the end of any day we cannot say that we have not enriched the life of another in at least some small way. The one who hoards is consumed with self; the one who cares, shares.

We should always feel blessed when we are able to stand in the serving side of the line rather than in the receiving side. In looking at the cause for a ruined life, we would have to diligently search for one that was caused by excessive giving. To take our eyes off ourselves and onto others will miraculously loosen the purse strings.

"The greatest gift is that which comes from the heart."

The world may think you are crazy for offering to give to one who is in need while your stockpile is dangerously low. But ignore them and give anyway. Heaven will be full of ones just like you.

Giving does not always involve money, though society has led us to believe that misconception. The greatest gift is that which comes from the heart. If each person would be willing to give a little, the world as a whole would get a lot. Just imagine the ramifications!

John A. James once said, *"One always receiving, never giving, is like the stagnant pool, in which whatever flows remains, whatever remains, corrupts."* Give and you receive; keep and you weep. The world seldom proclaims greatness to one who receives, but often to the one thoughtful and caring enough to give. I know what some of you are thinking; *"Oh give me a break!"* Surely, I need not remind you "it is more blessed to give than to receive."

*****

"Give, and it will be given to you. A good measure, pressed down, shaken together and running over, will be poured into your lap. For with the measure you use, it will be measured to you." [Luke 6:38]

20 - Did You Hear The Latest About...?

"I know you can keep a secret, so I don't mind telling you." The secret is, if someone says this to you, know that he or she is asking you to do something that they cannot do themselves. If they could, they wouldn't be telling you about it. Gossip is one of the most damaging types of behavior that exists because it is degrading and harmful. Now do not repeat this to anybody, but I personally believe that women are a bit more inclined to gossip than men are. (The reason I ask you not to repeat that is not so much that I don't want the rumor to spread, it's just that I don't want to get hurt by my wife, and others of the *sweeter, kinder, gentler* gender.) I might say, in my defense, that the main reason I believe this to be true is because I think, on the whole, women are much better communicators than men are. They have a tendency to actually listen when someone is speaking to them and therefore have more stored information from which to share. (How about it, ladies, "Have I added enough positive comments to outweigh the negative one?") Actually, it doesn't matter who spreads rumors more than the other. What matters is that it is not the nice thing to do. Nice? Who wants to be nice? *"Did you hear the latest about...?"*

For those who think the scripture reference from the latter part of Acts 20:35 - *"...it is more blessed to give than to receive."* - is referring to gossip, I have some bad news for you. The area of spreading rumors is one of the only places where this is not the truth. A gossip has been described as being the mail carrier for the devil, and I think this description comes pretty close to being accurate. Gossip receives no high marks in good citizenship because it does nothing to build others up.

I believe we should have a new penalty for gossipers and hearers of gossip. My plan is this: those who spread gossip should be hung by their tongues, and those who listen to it should be hung by their ears. I can almost guarantee you that if this were the case the amount of gossip would certainly decline. One of the down sides to a plan like this is that we would have a society full of people who went around with long droopy ears and tongues dragging the ground. On second thought, we had better not put this idea into practice, because we look silly enough the way it is.

I read somewhere that gossip is nothing more than halitosis of the mind. I would have to agree with that because it sure stinks when you stop to think about it. It is funny, but when something is being told about others, it is easy to take part in the listening. However, you let the personal tales start, and that is where the hurt is fully realized.

Gossip is nothing more than a "mouth trap" for the "rats" of life. One thing to remember about gossip is that the more interesting it is, the more unlikely it is to be true. For what happens with gossip is that each time it is told, it grows just a little bit more "appetizing" to the ear. We want to make sure it is nice and juicy, so we add our own flavoring to it. The problem is not what goes in one ear and out the other. The problem is what goes in one ear, gets mixed up in the brain, and then slips out through the mouth.

> *"Gossip is nothing more than a* **mouth trap** *for the rats of life."*

My advice for you is to stay away from those with "loose lips" and "itchy ears" or you, too, may become infected!

Epictetus is credited with having said, *"If you are such that one speaks ill of you, make no defense against what was said, but answer, 'He surely knew not of my other faults, else he would not have mentioned these only!'"*. Most of us who have been the victims of gossip could echo these words as well. We need to live our lives in such a way that we are not afraid of what our kids might say when they are having supper at the neighbors' house.

> *"It is true that three can keep a secret, but only if two are dead."*

Understand that if you spend time at work, either spreading gossip or listening to it, you are stealing from your employer because you are taking time away from doing your work. Now you may say, "Well, I just do it at break time." If that is the case, I say, *"Give me a break!"* Breaks are for taking breaks, not breaking the reputation of others.

Here is a good rule for life: "If you are not willing to write something down and sign your name to it, don't say it!" Again, I believe if this were practiced by everyone, we would have much less gossip than we do now.

"If you are not willing to write something down and sign your name to it, don't say it!"

If you tell someone something that a little bird told you, make sure it wasn't from a cuckoo or a dodo bird. One of the hardest things to try to do is to stop a rumor. It is much like trying to "un-ring" a bell. Gossip is nothing more than "ear pollution," coming from a newscaster who has no credibility.

It is amazing that a three-inch tongue has enough poison in it to kill many people. Therefore, we need to make sure that we keep ours under lock and key at all times. There is one thing that puzzles me about rumors: How in the world can they travel so fast when they don't have a leg to stand on? Makes you wonder if they aren't being carried along by others, doesn't it?

It is true that three people can keep a secret, but only if two of them are dead. Speaking of three, I would like to leave you with three rules for healthy teeth: 1. Brush after every meal 2. Visit your dentist twice a year. 3. Mind your own business.

That reminds me, I need to go brush and floss, but before I do, *"Did you hear the latest about...?"*

*****

"Like a club or a sword or a sharp arrow is the man who gives false testimony against his neighbor." [Proverbs 25:18]

21 - Happy Hour

Iam not sure which restaurant holds claim to the original "Happy Hour," but whichever one it was, they missed the mark in my book. I feel sure the concept was originated by someone who noticed the money intake was not as great during the hours from four to seven p.m. and tried to think of an ingenious way to convince people to part with more of their hard-earned money. What better way than to offer "happiness" as the result? Most people will do anything to make themselves happy, will they not? However, one thing they forgot to tell us is that you cannot buy happiness; it does not come bottled up with a lid on it. The only true container of happiness is the heart.

Something else that bothers me in regard to *"Happy Hour"* is this: since when does 4 to 7 equal one hour? Give me a break!

True happiness is more a way of life than something to shoot for. It is more a permanent resident of the mind than an occasional visitor. Another interesting fact is that it seldom travels alone because it has two friends - cheerfulness and kindness. Happiness is what resides within us when we give selfishness the eviction notice. Happiness is the award we receive for serving others.

"The only true container of happiness is the heart"

Most of us are concerned about the legacy we will leave when we are gone, and what will be left to pass onto future generations. Happiness is one heirloom that can be enjoyed for the here and now and for the hereafter as well. We just need to discipline ourselves in the areas of faith, hope and love.

If happiness is the "self-fulfilling" target at which you aim, you are pointing in the wrong direction. Look for ways to enrich the lives of others, and you will bag your limit every time. Many are they who miss the mark when aiming for happiness because their focus in on the "I" in "dead" center. Happiness is in the habit of chasing the heart that is always willing to help others.

Pleasure and happiness are sometimes mistaken for twins, but it's certain that they are not identical. Pleasures are much faster and many times short-lived, whereas true happiness should be a lifelong companion.

A moment of happiness holds more reason for living than a lifetime of selfishness. For selfishness is the seed from which foolishness grows. To reap a harvest of happiness, make sure you are sowing seeds of kindness. It is no coincidence that the heart full of happiness is part of the same body that has helping hands. Contrary to popular belief, happiness is not the result of doing what you like, but liking what you do. Our happiness is dependent upon the thoughts we allow to enter our minds. Is it time for a "changing of the guards"?

Everyone enters the race in which happiness is the medal, but some become discouraged and drop out before reaching the finish line. Happiness can be pursued but is only caught as a by-product of serving others. The best starting point in the chase for happiness is at the line of helpfulness. Ready, set, go!

You are fearfully and wonderfully made, and the instruction manual clearly states that you must "forget self" and find ways to bless others. Otherwise, the warranty is null and void.

"A moment of happiness holds more reason for living than a lifetime of selfishness."

As we pack for our journey through life, let's be sure we put in extra gentleness, kindness and self-control. Then when we look back at the photos we have taken, we will notice that we are wearing a smile. As we observe nature and the marvel of the animal kingdom, it sometimes appears that we humans are the only species to have been absent during the lesson on how to live a joy filled life. If you do not believe me, take the time to listen to the songs of the birds or watch a puppy propel his tail at the sight of his master. If a man has lost all happiness, when someone sees him coming their way, they may appropriately yell, "Dead man walking!"

As Christians, our job description clearly states that we are to do whatever the boss commands, and if that means working overtime and missing the world's so-called "Happy Hour," so be it. Why should we even entertain the idea of shortchanging ourselves and limit it to just one hour, or three or whatever length of time *"Happy Hour"* is supposed to last? Wouldn't you rather be a founding member of *"Happy Life"*?

*****

"A cheerful heart is good medicine, but a crushed spirit dries up the bones." [Proverbs 17:22]

22 - Hope Will Leave The Light On For You!

Most if not all of us have found ourselves in the position of feeling as if we were at the end of our rope and could sense our grip slipping away. It is a fact of life that issues will come and bring drops of darkness and despair with them. But that is the beautiful thing about hope. *"Hope will leave the light on for you"* when the rest of the world looks dark.

Only a fool can scoff at the power of hope, because those who have experienced it know what strength it brings. A single thread of hope does more to hold life together than all the cords of conflict. Hope puts doubt in its place and gives one the assurance that the best is yet to come. Hope is a friend who will hold your hands through the dark alleys of the world.

Hope has a way of taking fear by the scruff of the neck and letting it know who is in charge. Some will tell you that hope is hopeless when faced with certain tragedy. I say hope can make certain tragedy change its mind when it sees both you and hope ready to do battle. Hope is the springtime of the soul, bringing with it the delights of new life and the dreams of new fruit, soon to be harvested.

"Hope is the great physician for the ills of despair."

The hope we carry in ourselves can be used to encourage others through tough times and enable them to continue on until they find hope of their own. Every heart should hold ample hope, in that it has plenty to share with others, and yet not find its own cupboard bare. Hope is the strength to go on when the world is yelling, **"Stop!"**

Fear is the natural enemy of hope. However, when fear sees hope coming over the hill with its head held high, fear tucks tail and runs. Hope is the great physician for the ills of despair.

Elbert Hubbard once said, *"Parties who want milk should not seat themselves on a stool in the middle of a field in hope that the cow will back up to them."* Nevertheless, to Mr. Hubbard I say, *"The chances of a cow appearing in the middle of the field are still way ahead of one showing up for someone still sitting at the table."* It is true that hope alone will accomplish little if it is not harnessed with animals of action. For hope gives reason to everyone but fruition only to those who act.

Hope has turned the heads of many and prevented them from running into the walls of woe. The expectation of tomorrow can be the tonic for today's troubles. Hope gives wings to our faith and allows it to float overhead, putting things in their proper perspective.

Hope has also been the foothold for many a man to move forward. Hope is a combination of dreaming and expecting that dream to come true soon. Every new day brings hope with it.

A single star of hope can give a darkened night a reason to hang on until dawn. Hope offers us something to believe in. It gives us assurance that the present difficulty will soon be a thing of the past. Hope has a way of bringing head and heart together so their owner can retain the desire to move on with life. A soul without hope is a desolate place. However, a soul that brings hope to the one without will be considered an oasis of refreshment.

> *"A single star of hope can give a darkened night a reason to hold on until dawn."*

The hope of a better future has inspired many to grab hold of their dreams and take the necessary steps to fulfill them. Many times the level of greatness in a person is determined by the level of hope they pass onto their fellow man. Only a fool would put a price tag on the value of hope. Hope can build a fire in a heart that has lost its spark. When hope goes on leave, misery moves in!

A person without hope is "The Prince of Paupers" and has the knack for enlisting others to join his ranks. Hope brings happiness with it, but the length of stay for both depends on the warmth of the welcome.

It is better for a man to have an ounce of hope than a ton of doubt. Hope has been described as the "greatest of deceivers," but only by those who have none. As ridiculous as hope may look to those who do not know her, she is most beautiful to those who do.

> *"It is better to have an ounce of hope than a ton of doubt."*

Without hope, dreams die. Without dreams, men die. Without men, hope is never born. When man has breathed his last breath of hope, he is not long for this world. Even if he still exists and makes his presence known, he is but a corpse that moves.

Hope does not harbor prejudice, for she is often a houseguest in the pit of poverty as well as the palace of a prince. She will give a reason for living to anyone who will accept the invitation.

An Arabian proverb says, *"He who has health, has hope; and he who has hope has everything."* However, even when our health takes a turn for the worse, if hope stays around, we still have a reason to live.

In doing my research on hope, I came across a quote by Tom Bodett that is worth sharing. *"They say a person needs just three things to be truly happy in this world. Someone to love, something to do, and something to hope for."* No matter what you are facing in your life today, I want you to know, as Tom might say in one of his motel ads, *"Hope will leave the light on for you!"*

*****

"Therefore, since we have such a hope, we are very bold." [2 Corinthians 3:12]

23 - Hospitality Is A Hospital For All

True hospitality makes a person feel more like a member of the family than merely a guest. It has a way of saying, "What is mine, is yours," whereas the mere act of entertaining speaks without really saying, "What is mine is mine."

In the days of old, when travelers would venture away from home, they often found conditions to be less than desirable. Therefore, religious leaders of the day established international guesthouses as havens for weary souls. They were called "hospice," from the Latin word "hospes," meaning "guests." Hospice guests were shown kindness and offered assistance with other pressing needs when they visited. They actually became hospitals, if you will, for anyone with a special need while they were away from their own home. Even though the hospice centers of today exist with an economic agenda, originally they were a haven for guests, a place where one could go for comfort and kindness. For those of us who have been the recipients, I think we would have to agree, *"Hospitality is a hospital for all."*

*"Hospitality us more than just opening
your home to others;
it is opening your heart as well."*

Hospitality is more than just opening your home to others - it is opening your heart as well. It is an avenue to extend love to those you cherish, as well as those you have every reason to believe would not help you in your time of need. Hospitality comes easier with the proper perspective that God owns it all, and you are simply watching over it for him.

Hospitality means offering someone an environment where she feels free to be herself. A place where guests know they will be accepted, warts and all. It offers others a home away from home. Hospitality should restore faith, offer hope and be done with love.

There will be times when you would just rather leave your door locked and not fulfill the role of host or hostess, but it is in these difficult times that someone will be especially blessed - and many times it will be **you**, the one offering the hospitality. Many times acts of hospitality offer a chance to share food with one another, and at others, food for the spirit. In either case, nourishment is provided. An opportunity to offer hospitality is an opportunity to touch the life of another.

As I said in my opening paragraph, entertainment and hospitality are not the same. Entertainment provides, for personal reasons, a chance to flaunt what you have. While hospitality provides an opportunity to serve others, in large or small ways. The main difference therefore is the motive behind each.

"An opportunity to offer hospitality is an opportunity to touch the life of another."

True hospitality pays no attention to status level but makes each guest feel as if they were the guest of honor. It also offers an opportunity to be kind and loving, even to those who are not themselves. Through your offering of hospitality, some will take advantage, but be generous anyway. Being generous is good - being hospitable is being good and generous at the same time.

In being a good host or hostess, you should let everyone know that you are happy when they arrive and saddened when they leave. The house of the hospitable may not always be neat and orderly, but the welcome should be. To invite someone into your home shows trust and a willingness to do whatever possible to lighten another's load, even if only for a short period of time. Hospitality should be wrapped in kindness and offer an opportunity to strengthen existing friendships as well as develop new ones. It is a combination of generosity and friendship. When someone is in need, an ounce of hospitality is better than a pound of promises. Hospitality offers a welcome hand and a warm heart.

It should be our goal to help as many as we can on their journey through life, and therefore make our journey more enjoyable as well. Through hospitality, a bond begins between the host and/or hostess and the guest. It is one way of turning your home into a mission field. Gestures of hospitality are most rewarding when the purpose is simply to serve. Hospitality ceases to be hospitality when there are conditions attached.

Hospitality is not reserved for the wealthy; it's often best practiced by the poor. All you need is a willing heart to reach out to others and offer them a part of what you have been blessed with. Ironically, we need to be extra careful in not allowing prosperity to diminish our habit of being hospitable. The art of hospitality is just that, an art. And like most others, it's tried by many but mastered by few. However, do not allow that to discourage you, for with practice, you, too, can offer a haven for guests and provide a place for renewal. You will come to know and realize, *"Hospitality is a hospital for all."*

*****

"Offer hospitality to one another without grumbling." [1 Peter 4:9]

24 - You Think That's Funny, Don't You?

I have a large collection of joke books. As a matter of fact, my wife would probably tell you that I have so many that it isn't even funny. However, I am probably much like you in that I only wish I could remember half the jokes I have heard or read in my lifetime. To be honest with you, the other half have not been worth remembering, let alone repeating. I must share with you the fact that humor and jokes are not the same thing. Take life for example; it is no joke, but it still can be a humorous experience. In my mind, humor is an insurance policy against taking life too seriously. I believe that a sense of humor will do more to get you through life than a whole bucket of learning ever will. Humor can enable us to face each day with the knowledge that there will be things worth laughing at if we will simply look for them.

> *"...humor is an insurance policy against taking life too seriously."*

What would a chapter on humor be without at least one joke? Boring, to say the least, so here goes: The boss announced, "I've decided to use humor in the workplace. Experts say that humor eases tension, which is important at a time when the workforce is being trimmed. Knock knock."

The employee answered, "Who's there?"

To which the boss answered, "Not you anymore." What can I say except, *"You think that's funny, don't you?"*

To lack a sense of humor is to lead a miserable life and therefore cause those around you to do the same. Pity the poor person who cannot laugh at himself, for how dare him to laugh at others. A sense of humor is a staple in life's survival kit. Research has shown that laughter can be a cure for many ailments. With humor as your ally, you can face many enemies and win the wars. Humor can destroy panic and allow you to regain self-control. To cry can be good; to laugh can be better; to laugh until you cry is best. Humor is actually ammunition that can be used to defuse a situation that is about to explode.

A sense of humor leads to a sense of coping with circumstances, and making the best of a bad situation. The level of impact from any conflict is minimized by appropriate humor. An atmosphere of humor can give a breath of fresh air to an otherwise dark and dreary world. A sense of humor has a tendency to make the terrible tolerable. Laughter will lighten the load when given the chance.

Laughter is one of the main ingredients of life, and until you allow it the position it deserves, your world will remain endurable at best. Laughter is not saying that a situation is not serious, but is letting the situation know that it will not defeat us. Nothing is so grave in life that it cannot be eased with a sense of humor. Laughter can be a soothing ointment if applied with care and gentleness.

"A sense of humor is a staple in life's survival kit."

To have others laugh with us contributes little in the makeup of a person's character, but to be laughed at, and be able to continue smiling, speaks volumes. Each of us needs to give the world the right to amuse itself with our blunders, both now and when we die. A sense of humor allows our life to run smoother and longer. Laughter and longevity are related. A sense of humor, even if it does not add years to your life, will add life to your years. Jennifer James is credited with saying, *"If you choose one characteristic that would get you through life, choose a sense of humor."* It cannot do everything, but it can definitely do its part.

The number of friends you have is highly influenced by your sense of humor. People do not want to be around someone who cannot take, or take part in, a joke. A sense of humor should be our personal tank of "laughing gas." Make sure yours doesn't run out just when you need it the most. Humor is not funny to the one who has no sense of its worth. However, humor can be found in most any situation, if we look at the absurdity of it. When you have grown too old to laugh, you have already died!

Comedians are hard-pressed to make up humor that is even half as funny as the happenings of real life. Do yourself a favor and look for the funny side of life. It is difficult to stay too serious in the presence of humor. We also need to make sure our face knows when we think something is funny, and express our joy so others can see it, and even find humor in our expressions. Humor is there if we look for it.

"A sense of humor allows our life to run smoother and longer."

Humor is an excellent communicator; it can often teach a lesson that would be difficult to comprehend in any other way. Also, advice disguised as humor is more readily accepted than when it is presented as criticism. A sense of humor allows us to get a clear picture of just how absurd we are, and "That's funny - I don't care who you are!"

It is a proven fact that productivity will pick up in an environment into which fun's been invited. We do not have to look any farther than Southwest Airlines. Southwest seems to be the only airline that is able to make it on its own. I cannot help but attribute part of that to the fact that the employees know that it is OK to have fun at their job. And in making it fun for themselves, they make travel more bearable for their customers. You will discover that people are funny when they are allowed to be. Make sure you do not stifle the sense of humor of your co-workers - and most of all your own.

If I should err on one side or the other, let it be on the side of taking life too lightly, rather than too seriously. Life is far too short to be taken seriously. Few people are more miserable than those who lack a sense of humor. *"Now you think that's funny, don't you?"* Well, if you do, you need to work on your sense of humor!

*****

"A happy heart makes the face cheerful, but heartache crushes the spirit. The discerning heart seeks knowledge, but the mouth of a fool feeds on folly.

All the days of the oppressed are wretched, but the cheerful heart has a continual feast." [Proverbs 15:13-15]

25 - You Really Think I Should?

Integrity seems to be a rare commodity in our world today. It seems everyone is in it for him or herself. The other person needs to be on the lookout for himself.

I ask you, how much more pleasant would it be if we knew without a doubt that each person we dealt with was a person of integrity? We would not have to have our guard up, wondering how we were going to be taken advantage of this time. We could relax and know with assurance that the dealings were going to be fair for everyone involved. Integrity, my friend, is a choice, one that each of us has the power to make in our individual lives. However, we sometimes are afraid to practice it ourselves for fear that we will be taken as a fool. Let me assure you that it is far better to be a fool with integrity than a rich man with no morals. Integrity is strength that comes from within. It is not subject to change; it does not succumb to outside forces. If integrity is not steadfast, it does not qualify as integrity. If you ever find yourself asking, *"You really think I should?"* the answer is most probably a resounding *"NO!"* unless, of course, you are a person of integrity, and then I would have to scream, *"GO FOR IT!"*

"...it is far better to be a fool with integrity than a rich man with no morals."

Integrity does not take advantage of others but looks out for their well-being as well as one's own. Values put into practice through our performance will speak volumes in reflecting the value of our values. In living a life of integrity, it is vitally important that we care about others and they know they can trust us to be committed to their best interests. Do the best you can each and every day, and people will know what to expect when dealing with you. Integrity should never feel cheated when you deal with someone who took advantage of you, as long as yours wasn't compromised. The surest way of building a business or a relationship is through strict integrity. Doing the right thing even when it is not expected is integrity - it should make no difference who is watching us.

If you are ever forced to choose between your career and compromising your integrity, do yourself a favor and choose integrity. There will always be someone else looking for a person of your quality, and you will be able to live with yourself. Integrity leaves no room for questions. If you have it, you have it; if you don't, you don't! With integrity as a quality, alibis are never necessary.

"With integrity as a quality, alibis are never necessary."

Two friends, Jerry and Frank, were talking as they walked down the road. Jerry said, "The grocer gave me a counterfeit dollar this morning. You can't trust anyone these days." Frank said, "Let me take a look at it." To which Jerry replied, "I can't. I passed it along at the drug store."

If we are to preach honesty as being the best policy, we must always practice it ourselves, or we preach falsehood. A hypocrite's philosophy in life is to tell the truth, even if it is a lie. Being a little crooked is a lot like being a little pregnant; there is no such thing!

In doing good for others, we do well for ourselves. In doing bad toward others, we treat ourselves far worse. It is a fact that the truth will set you free, but integrity means you were never in bondage to start with. The consequences of integrity are always tasty and palatable. When a person of integrity says they will, they will. And you can take it to the bank.

Integrity means making the right choice even when another would have benefited you more financially. In living a life of integrity, we must first be true to ourselves, and then it comes easy to be true to others. If we only put our best foot forward when it is convenient, we cripple our integrity. Living a life of integrity allows one to travel "First Class" every time, because when a person stays true to his word, his word goes up in value. Truth that is tainted is no truth at all, just a lie in disguise. To compromise one's integrity in order to win the favor of another is to lose big time!

"Truth that is tainted is no truth at all, just a lie in disguise."

If there is one gift that we could give our children that would prove to be their greatest asset in life, it would be the gift of integrity. For the grandest legacy anyone can hope to leave when he or she dies is for others to say, "This was a person of integrity."

A man read a classified ad in the newspaper that promised a cord of firewood for $40, including delivery and stacking. He figured he couldn't do it himself for that price, so he responded to the ad. When the other guy had finished unloading the truck and getting the wood all stacked, the buyer realized that the so-called "cord" of wood was way short of being what it should have. He told the guy about his concern, and the man answered, "Well, that's what I call a cord." Not wishing to argue, the customer opened his wallet, took out a $20 bill, and laid it in the man's hand. He immediately protested, and stated, "Hey, that's not $40!" The buyer was quick to reply with, "That's what I call $40!" Just because the majority of people say something is so, does not make it so.

Integrity is what holds our life together, and it makes us the same tomorrow as we were today. Compromise your integrity even once, and it stops being integrity. Henry Ford said, *"You can't build a reputation on what you are going to do."* If we are hoping to build a reputation of integrity, we must do more than hope; we must put it into use in every interaction.

There are always two choices, two paths that a person can take. One is easy, and its only reward is that it is easy. I am not sure who to give credit for the saying, *"There is no right way to do something wrong,"* but whoever was the first to utter those words was right on. Keeping that in mind, you be the judge when you hear yourself say, *"You really think I should?"*

*****

"May integrity and uprightness protect me, because my hope is in you." [Psalm 25:21]

26 - Are You Listening To Me?

A story is told of President Franklin D. Roosevelt, that he tired of smiling and saying nice things to people who really weren't listening to him as they came through greeting lines at White House receptions. One evening he decided to find out for himself if his suspicions of people not paying attention were true or not. Instead of smiling and saying the usual niceties, he'd put on the usual charming smile but follow it with the statement, "I murdered my grandmother this morning." Just as he thought, everyone would smile in return and say things like, "How nice. Just keep up the great work." It seemed that no one was listening to him until a foreign diplomat came through the line. When the president said, "I murdered my grand-mother this morning," the tactful diplomat bent over and softly said, "Mr. President, I am sure she had it coming!"

An amusing story for sure, but one that does make the point that people in general make much better talkers than listeners. Listening does not come as easily as one might think, and the truth is that few, if any, of us are as good at it as we would like to believe. Being a good listener is one of the surest ways to be considered considerate. You can win the heart of the one to whom you lend your ears.

When we are talking, we have a terrible time learning. When we truly listen, we have a tough time not learning. David Schwartz once said, *"Big people monopolize the listening. Small people monopolize the talking."* A skilled listener has a magnetic force that draws people to his side of the room.

Thoughts worth thinking often enter the mind through open ears but never through an open mouth. Listen to learn, and learn to listen, especially when you have the feeling that you already know what is going to be said. More times than not, you will be surprised. We must be a good listener, but the wisdom to rightfully distinguish what is worth listening to is far more important.

It is funny how we insist on the right to free speech, but never the right to listen. Many times, when people ask for our advice, they simply want us to listen to what they have to say, and agree with it.

Have you ever had a conversation with someone who answered your question before you finished asking it? To answer or interrupt before listening is the sign of a prophet or a fool. I am here to tell you that prophets are rare.

One pair of ears can easily tire a dozen tongues. Persuasion packs a powerful punch through a set of listening ears.

"One pair of ears can easily tire a dozen tongues."

It is a fact that "hard of hearing" and "just not listening" are two completely different issues. I heard a joke one time about two men talking to each other. The first man made the statement that his wife talked to herself a lot. The second man said that his did too, but she just didn't know it because she thought he was listening.

The wisest words ever spoken require listening ears to receive the message, or they are but folly. Demanding the right to speak and not valuing the chance to listen has been the downfall of many men and women.

"Good conversation involves more than talking."

If we can bring ourselves to encourage someone to elaborate when we think we have heard more than enough already, we not only have a chance of learning something, we have the chance to win a friend.

The formula to be more successful in almost any endeavor is to listen more. More sales are made by good listening than by good talking. And how many sales have been lost because the salesperson did not know when to stop talking? Nobody knows. Ironically, more times than not, the one who remains silent says something worth listening to.

Good conversation involves more than talking. Listening plays just as big a role - one that most people hope the other one will volunteer for.

The trouble with thinking twice before you speak is that you will have a tough time getting in on the conversation. "Did you hear what I said?" *"Are you listening to me?"*

*****

"Listen to me, you islands; hear this, you distant nations: Before I was born the Lord called me; from my birth he has made mention of my name." [Isaiah 49:1]

27 - All You Need Is Love

There are few, if any, subjects, on which there has been more written than love. Many claim to be experts when it comes to knowing what it is all about, but most of us realize that we know very little, except that we want more of it. The effects of it reach farther and deeper than we can imagine. If there is a stronger emotion than love, it has not yet made itself known. I sincerely believe that if there is one thing the entire world needs, it is love!

I came across a Swedish proverb that speaks volumes about how we should live our lives. *"Fear less, hope more; eat less, chew more; whine less, breathe more; talk less, say more; hate less, love more; and all good things are yours."* If we can just follow this advice, we will find ourselves well on our way to living life as it should be.

"Loves effects last a lifetime."

We are born as a receptacle for receiving love, as well as an everlasting source for supplying love. But sometimes we get short-circuited and love loses its way. Our entire world goes dark. Love's main purpose is to bring life, not only to its owner, but also to those with whom it is shared.

Love is forever. You cannot trace its beginning except to the heart of God, and neither can you visualize its ending, for it has no such thing. Love's effects last a lifetime.

A life cannot be a life of abundance unless love is at the center. Learning to love and learning to live are one in the same. A life in which love has no place is nothing more than a living coffin. To miss the mark and fail to love is certain death. Whatever the cost of love, be willing to pay the price.

Love does not have to be perfect to be the perfect solution. A heart of love is a heart of forgiving. Forgiveness can never become a reality until love takes hold. To speak of love as being wasted is to speak foolishly. Granted, it could have been more appropriately received, but trust me, some good was achieved. Try as you might, you cannot keep love hidden for long, as it will show itself in ways too bold to be missed.

Love is the fountain of youth. Although it may forget to tell your body, your heart knows full well, and will stay young forever. Love is a healer unlike any other, and can bring life to a heart that is dead. Show me a heart that has no love, and I will show you a heart of steel. Love cannot live where it is not permitted to permeate and grow. A life without love will echo from the hollowness of it.

Just as water sustains life in the physical world, love does the same for the soul. It is the key that unlocks all the beauty of this life, and gives one a reason to live. The true worth of a person's life can be measured in the moments of unselfishness that were used as opportunities to help others. Love has a way of taking a life filled with feelings of uselessness and making it realize its true worth. It can transform ugly to beautiful in just a matter of minutes.

To look back on your life and see moments when you failed the test of love, for those you should feel the most shame. A world where love is not exchanged is a world where war is wagered, and you will find that no one stands in the Winner's Circle. However, to have love in your life without the presence of anything else still makes for a full life.

"Love is the fountain of youth."

Love cannot control itself, and it's been known to overpower the hardest of hearts. The worth of a life cannot be worth much unless love has touched the hem of its garment. To love only the lovable is but a shadow of love. To extend it to those undeserving is love for real. Love can make a sane man wild with passion and a wild man sane with peace. When love comes calling, welcome it with open arms, and enjoy the benefits it brings. Love is not in the habit of finding fault but sees the possibility that lies within.

Love opens avenues of learning like no other virtue. For with it, your words are valued, and without it, your words are void. Once love grabs hold of you, it will lead you to places you never knew existed. Enjoy the ride!

To have respect for and to have love for, are two different things indeed. To respect, you hold at arm's length; to love is to wrap your arms around. The most important lesson any parent could teach their child (and the world benefits the most) is how to love. Life is seasoned with sprinkles of love; the more you sprinkle, the better the flavor.

A sharp tongue is a sign of a dull mind in control of it. Love and selfishness cannot live in the same room. For any love relationship to flourish, grow and bear fruit, all who are involved must nurture it.

For love to be extended and not be accepted is a slap in the face. Extend it anyway. For we remember the truth from the song of decades past, *"All you need is love!"*

*****

"Dear friends, let us love one another, for love comes from God. Everyone who loves has been born of God and knows God. Whoever does not love does not know God, because God is love." [1 John 4:7-8]

28 - Let's Crank That Baby Up!

Have you ever known someone so intent on achieving their life's dream that they were able to overcome tremendous difficulties and finally realize what they worked so hard for? History is full of them, and when we hear about people like this, it gives us hope and helps us believe that we can have the same outcome. The good news is, we can! The bad news is, you, and only you, must accept full responsibility for seeing that it happens. Oh, we can point fingers at excuses, but it does absolutely no good. When all is said and done, most people do exactly what they want to do, and nothing more. If they don't want to be motivated, then there is little that anyone else can do to change that fact. Motivation is the direct result of making up our minds we want something, and deciding to sacrifice whatever is necessary to achieve it. You have the power; do you have the desire? If so, *"Let's crank that baby up!"* and see what happens.

The desire to have something different or be something different from what is now reality gives us the motivation to pursue that desire. We have the final say in deciding whether we take action or do nothing. Motivation is - and always has been - an "inside job."

"Motivation is, and always has been an inside *job."*

I remember reading the story of Enrico Caruso, the world-famous tenor, and the opening night jitters that almost did him in. He was backstage, waiting in the wings to take his place and perform, when he began saying, "Get out of my way! Get out of my way!" The stagehands thought he was going crazy because there was no one even close to him, let alone blocking his way. Later, after a grand performance he explained, "I was just talking to the little me that was saying, 'I can't!' The big me inside, the one that knew I could, was saying 'Get out of my way!' You see, sometimes we need to let someone know who is in charge."

The defining moment is when we decide that we want something badly enough to make the sacrifices and concessions to make it happen. Our level of motivation is dependent on how well we can sell ourselves on the idea that we cannot live without it! Determine exactly what you want and focus your actions on achieving it, and it will soon be yours.

The reason it is so difficult to make a permanent change in our life is that we fail to focus our attention and energy on making the change a reality. If a person does not believe in his or her heart that they are deserving of a better life, seldom will they have one. The only way to get a person to better himself or herself is to paint them a picture of the possibility. Motivation is "want to" put into action.

A person is more willing to accept words of encouragement as a means of motivation if they coincide with what they want. The "want to" has to lead the way for the "will to." Once you make the right choice and allow the "want to" to do the leading, things will happen for the better. Helping a person discover their own strengths will do more to motivate than anything else you can do.

"Motivation is <u>want to</u> put into action."

Wake a person up from his sleep, and he will complain. Wake a person up to his potential, and he will praise. To get people to make changes in their life, they first must make the discovery that they don't like some part of the way it is now. This is only done through self-observation, for if another points it out to them, it is nothing more than heresy. Edgar A. Guest had some great advice: *"Give the man you'd like to be a look at the man you are."* When you do that, the realization of needed change will be evident. The point at which a person decides to quit playing the game of life and to start taking it seriously is the point at which motivation kicks in. However, you must be sure that what you want is what *you* want, and not something that someone else wants for you. The decision is yours!

It is sickening to lie to others, but downright deadly to lie to self. Stop telling yourself that you cannot do something, and take the steps toward doing just that thing. William Shakespeare's famous words, *"This above all: to thine own self be true."* is right on! It is honorable to be honest with others but essential that we are honest with ourselves. When a person makes up their mind as to exactly what it is they want out of life, they find the decisions on where to spend their efforts become easier to make.

"It is sickening to lie to others, but down right deadly to lie to self."

When you realize that what you think of yourself is far more important that what others think, you will be free to pursue the dreams of your soul. A true picture of one's self will reveal the fact that you are who you are, and where you are in life, because of the choices you have made. Also, take note that you have the only vote that counts when deciding what you will do from now on. To be a success, you must first be motivated!

The reason you haven't changed your life before now is because you didn't care if you did or not. Find yourself, and you will have made a great discovery indeed. This should be top priority for every man and woman. So what about it? Are you ready? Well then, *"Let's crank that baby up!"*

*****

"Let us not become weary in doing good, for at the proper time we will reap a harvest if we do not give up. Therefore, as we have opportunity, let us do good to all people, especially to those who belong to the family of believers." [Galatians 6:9-10]

29 - Half Full or Half Empty?

We usually find exactly what we are looking for, do we not? We must constantly be aware of our minds and where we allow our thoughts to lead us, or we may find ourselves stuck in some rut rather than on the road we wish to travel.

The pessimist sees what is wrong with any given situation; the optimist is busy looking for what is best. The pessimist is looking for someone to feel sorry for him; the optimist is busy spreading joy. The pessimist is finding fault; the optimist finds favor. The pessimist is griping about the seeds in his fruit; the optimist is busy gathering them to plant and envisioning more bounty. The pessimist thinks of how bad things are; the optimist is giving thanks for the blessings of life. The pessimist complains; the optimist encourages. The pessimist builds walls of loneliness; the optimist fuels friendships. The pessimist makes his meal of misery; the optimist is fed with favor. The pessimist is busy building barriers; the optimist occupied with opening the way.

When we consider the winds that blow through life, the optimist wonders how high his kite can fly while the pessimist is worried about how soon his will fall.

Have you ever considered the fact that you cannot gripe and be grateful at the same time? In fact, thankfulness and touchiness are not found together either. In addition, if you should ever find yourself with feelings of pessimism, try praying because the two are never compatible.

The smile on our face is the bloom that stems from the seeds of optimism. In addition, an optimist pays more attention to the flower that blooms than to the thorns that thrive. When an optimist smells flowers, he looks around for the wedding; the pessimist for the funeral. Moreover, when it rains, do you look for the rainbow, or are you more perturbed by the puddles? An optimist enjoys sunshine instead of shadows, and gladness instead of gloom. It is not surprising that the door of opportunity opens more than occasionally for the optimist.

> *"The smile on our face is the bloom that stems from the seeds of optimism."*

Whether we look at it as taking a chance or reaching for a golden opportunity determines how we make our approach; sneaking or standing upright. If we are observant, we will discover that every day wears clothing with pockets of possibilities.

The optimist habitually takes deep breaths of life, as he understands there is an abundance of fresh air. He thinks big, knowing he sets his own limits (see Philippians 4:13). And he chooses his words from the quill of kindness, understanding that the discouraged are desperate for a shot of hope. The optimist builds his dwelling on the Isle of Opportunity, but the pessimist finds himself stranded in the Sea of Sarcasm.

*"An optimist enjoys sunshine instead of shadows,
and gladness instead of gloom."*

The pessimist is quick to whine about why something will not work, while the optimist is busy praising prosperity and its source. An optimist is someone who tackles a task that most consider impossible, with enthusiasm, excitement and endless dreams of what is possible. While the pessimist is busy getting his degree in errors, enemies and evils, the optimist graduates with honors in ability, aplenty and affirmation. The question each of us must ask is, "Where is my diploma coming from?"

As Christians, it is our job to look for humor in the serious, to find joy in adversity, the good in the bad, and the strength in those the world considers weak.

*****

"Do not let any unwholesome talk come out of your mouths, but only what is helpful for building others up according to their needs, that it may benefit those who listen." [Ephesians 4:29]

30 - It's Always Too Soon To Quit

E ver felt like throwing your hands into the air and saying, "I quit!"? Maybe you have not only felt like it, maybe you did. And who is to blame you? If they had suffered what you have suffered, most would have done the same thing.

Most is the word I want you to catch in that sentence. Notice I didn't say **All**. For if **all** had quit, nothing more would have ever been accomplished than that which would equal your achievements. It is imperative that you not give up when faced with knockdowns and knots, because to win most battles, you do not have to be more powerful than your opponent, just more persistent. To endure is to earn bragging rights. What the world is saying can't be done is being accomplished everyday with perspiration and persistence. Every accomplishment, whether great or small, save those laden with luck, has come about because of the ability to stay focused and undaunted by disappointment.

"To endure is to earn bragging rights."

If we can muster the might to wade through the puddles of everyday living, we will eventually find ourselves standing above the water at the helm of the ship. If we are truly devoted to making our dreams become reality, we will trudge on no matter how many trials we encounter. There seems to be a hidden power that ensures everyone success if they simply stay with the task at hand. Amid all the greatest inventions, not one exists that will give us instant success. We must be willing to persevere and make adjustments from our last attempt. To make one's mind up not to grow weary under the burden of setbacks is to ensure success.

To persevere does not mean you will always win the race, but it does mean you will finish. Do not allow doom to dampen your spirits. It assures you of at least another shot at the title the next time. Nothing worth having ever comes easy except maybe the chance to try again. To follow through until a task is conquered allows us to taste victory and the reward of rest, sweet rest. The only true failure is the quitter.

Calvin Coolidge said it very eloquently: *"Nothing in the world can take the place of persistence. Talent will not; nothing is more common than unsuccessful men with talent. Genius will not; unrewarded genius is almost a proverb. Education will not; the world is full of educated derelicts. Persistence and determination alone are omnipotent."*

"The only true failure is the quitter."

Upon close examination, one will discover that success came to work everyday dressed in work clothes. If by chance "Plan A" doesn't work, make sure you have a "Plan B" to fall back on. If opportunity does present itself, at least you have direction for continuing. Refuse to allow your final destiny to be "down and out." When others quit, give it one more shot at going "up and in." We will discover that perseverance packs a more powerful punch than power itself.

No matter how well we point the gun, if we have failed to load it with appropriate ammunition, we are dead! We must prepare before we go into battle with guns ablazing. To fall short in the area of preparation sets us up to fail.

The one quality that is present in everyone who succeeds is perseverance. Without it, victories are left unclaimed, just one step from the finish line. Of course, the way to winning will not always be smooth sailing. But the victor will be the one who is able to catch another breath of air when the ways of the world have knocked the wind from others sails. Nevertheless, as long as we understand that *falling* is not failing, and failing is not *fatal*, we will survive.

"The way to winning will not always be smooth sailing."

To allow ourselves to be blinded by the rays of disappointment will prevent us from seeing our goals fulfilled. To move forward, a person must continue to act upon their beliefs even when logic tells them to stop. We must understand that "persistence pays." It even hands out bonuses to those who stay around for the party!

Hey! You! Where do you think you are going? This fight is just about to start; if you don't show up, how can you expect to win?

*****

"And here is my advice about what is best for you in this matter: Last year you were the first not only to give but also to have the desire to do so. Now finish the work, so that your eager willingness to do it will be matched by your completion of it, according to your means." [2 Corinthians 8:10-11]

31 - Praise The Lord And Pass The Biscuits!

I am assured that if the call were made to form two lines - one for those who had received too many words of appreciation and sincere praise in their life, and another for those who had room for more - it would be very lopsided. We all like to receive words of encouragement, do we not? In fact, it seems to come as standard equipment for all of us. The only words of caution to go along with the plea to praise is to make sure your motive is right and that the praise is deserved. Giving words of praise where they are not appropriate is an injustice to all involved. There is a tremendous difference between praise and flattery; one is done for the good of self, and the other for the uplifting of others. So, with that in mind, praise on. As a matter of fact, *"Praise the Lord and pass the biscuits!"*

Praise gives nourishment and life-sustaining nutrients to the heart and soul. Praise is to the heart as a vitamin is to the body. Praise offers the little "extra" that is needed to get one through the day. Words of appreciation are "miracle-grow" for seeds planted in the mind. It is amazing how much positive energy is generated in the heart and mind of one who knows that someone believes in them. The need to be appreciated is just as important in keeping one going as the food we eat. Actually, we could have just eaten a full-course meal, and the craving for appreciation would still linger.

"Praise is to the heart as a vitamin is to the body."

Happiness doesn't come from the possession of material things but from knowing that our fellow man thinks we are of worth. Want to be invited into a person's heart? Words of love and kindness will unlock all doors and swing them wide open for your grand entrance. By letting a person know you appreciate them for who they are, you enable them to grow into something more. For praise is automatically accompanied by a new standard of acceptance in the one on the receiving end, and they will do their best to meet it.

Even though it cannot be used to pay the bills, appreciation is the most gratifying means of reimbursement a worker can receive. The level of productivity goes up in direct proportion to the level of praise given. People will give the best they have and hold nothing in reserve when you praise them and respect them for who they are. To look for the best in another and praise them for their performance will inspire them to give it their all. If we see and treat a person as great potential rather than a problem, they will do their best to become so.

Everyone is inspired and enlightened by sincere praise and becomes a better person for it - if they let it go to their heart and not to their head. Praise can be a blessing or a curse, depending on what the receiver does with it. If it encourages and gives the desire to do even better in the future, it is a blessing indeed. If it puffs one up and instills a feeling of superiority, it is among the worst of gifts. President Dwight D. Eisenhower once said, *"Sweet praise is like perfume. It is fine if you don't swallow it."* Nevertheless, the level of humility has no say in whether people feel good upon hearing sincere words of appreciation, for all men do.

A person greedy for compliments is usually looking for handouts for something they have never earned. If we praise everyone for everything, our praise is worth nothing. Unearned praise does not carry the same impact as that for which one has done duty.

Few, if any, prefer sincere criticism as much as they do a compliment; it does not matter whether the compliment is sincere or not.

A man or woman is seldom despised for sharing sincere words of praise and appreciation, unless it comes from an enemy of the recipient. Moreover, most of us do not like interruptions, unless, of course, it is to allow applause for our efforts. A wise person accepts praises given, but only believes a part of them. They do the same with any criticism they may receive.

It is not a compliment - as a matter of fact it is an insult - to praise the merits of another in one breath and then say "Except…" in the next. It is a good idea to let people know exactly what it is you are praising them for, so it will not be mistaken as flattery.

> **"Praise is the sunlight for the soul, and all need it to grow."**

An appropriate touch or hug can speak volumes of praise without ever saying a word. In addition, a smile is another way to say a silent word of encouragement. However, if you should ever want to check another person's hearing, just whisper words of praise about them, and you will be amazed at how well they can hear. Praise is sunlight for the soul, and all need it to grow. Therefore, if you desire your world to have more sunshine and joy in it, make sure you sow appropriate seeds as you greet others. A compliment costs nothing but pays great dividends.

In sharing praise, we must always remember to give praise to the Lord of our lives, first and foremost. For it is His desire that we do so. He hungers for it as we all do. So with that in mind, allow me to say, *"Praise the Lord and pass the biscuits!"*

*****

"For as the soil makes the sprout come up and a garden causes seeds to grow, so the Sovereign Lord will make righteousness and praise spring up before all nations." [Isaiah 61:11]

32 - You Think You've Got Problems!

Problems are a part of everyone's life. Some of us have a problem. Some of us live with a problem. And some of us are the problem.

Lets be honest. Every life has its own set of problems. However, one of the worst things we can do when we face a problem is to stick our heads in the proverbial sand and pretend that it doesn't exist. It's like the story of the battered and bruised boxer hearing his trainer say between rounds, "You're looking good out there kid! He's barely laid a glove on you." To which the kid replied, "Well, then, you had better keep a closer eye on the referee, because somebody in this ring is beating the stuffing out of me!"

"Life comes at us from all directions."

I am sure that some of you who are reading this can relate to the kid at this point in your life. It feels like somebody just gave you an upper cut to the jaw. It could be almost anything, because life has a way of creeping up on you, and when you least expect it, drop the hammer on you, full-force. Life comes at us from all directions. We must learn to make the best of whatever the situation, no matter what it might be. Hoping it was not so will not change it one bit. We must take hold of the problem and make changes that we believe will steer things back in the direction we wish life to go. I believe the best position in which to perform these tasks is on your knees, with your eyes closed and head bowed.

Many are they who complain of their problems, but few are willing to exchange them with someone else, for fear of what the new set of problems might hold. "Into every life a little rain must fall." Sometimes it is a sprinkle, and sometimes it is an all-out flood! No matter the magnitude nor the fortitude of a problem, we must take steps, no matter how small, toward finding a workable solution. If we will continue to do that, eventually we will either have solved it, or have a hold on it that enables us to control it, and not vice- versa.

Malcomb Forbes said, *"When things are bad, we take a bit of comfort in the thought that they could always be worse. And when they are, we find hope in the thought that things are so bad they have to get better."*

I used to be a bit of a whiner. My wife reminded me of it occasionally, so I promised to stop. Now I don't whine, I just state facts! [Linda is having a bit of a problem herself, trying to figure out the difference. She says my facts now sound an awful lot like the whining I used to do. Imagine that!] I have concluded that whining never solved anyone's problems, but occasionally it does a person good just to ventilate. However, there is one rule about whining that needs to be heeded, and it's this: "Always make sure no one else is within hearing distance."

"The less one knows about the problem, the more solutions they have to offer."

I believe that some problems are placed in our lives to allow us to focus on our blessings. They do seem to offer that option if we would just take the time to look.

Each of us has our own problems, but pity the person who cannot forget his own long enough to help a friend cope with theirs. In sharing our problems with those around us, we run the risk of bringing them down as well. It takes a special caliber of people to lift you up to their level. We refer to these people as "friends." To help solve the problems of others, it often requires us to take a long walk in their shoes.

"Most problems shrink in the face of confrontation."

Most problems shrink in the face of confrontation. The best way to solve a problem is to break it down into bite-sized chunks, and eat away! There is seldom only one solution to any problem. So keep an open mind and a readiness to react. For when we turn our backs on our problems, their shadows will hide our sunshine.

J.C. Penney said, *"I am grateful for all my problems. After each one was overcome, I became stronger and more able to meet those that were still to come. I grew in all my difficulties."* With an attitude like that, problems become bearable. Problems can be problems or possibilities; every life has plenty of both.

Most, if not all, problems have "neglect" in their genes. If we will take the time to analyze and dissect them, we can usually learn and benefit from finding out how we could have prevented many from ever being born.

During a sale at the local auction barn, proceedings were halted and the auctioneer announced, "A fellow in the room has lost his wallet containing one thousand dollars.

He is offering two hundred dollars for its return." Then came a voice from the rear: "Two hundred and ten!"

And *"you think you have problems!"*

*****

> *"And we know that in all things God works for the good of those who love him, who have been called according to his purpose."* [Romans 8:28]

33 - Quality Never Grows Old

I don't know about you, but it seems to me that our society today, as a whole, is more concerned about the price of something than the quality of it. Oh, of course, we would all like to have our cake and eat it, too, as the old saying goes. However, finding a product that is offered at a good price and yet has quality built into it is a rare find indeed. The price of a product is usually a good indicator of the amount of quality that has gone into it. I am a firm believer that a consumer is willing to pay for quality, if they are assured it is honestly presented. Take myself for instance. Just last evening I made a trip to the store to purchase a set of measuring spoons to replace ones that I had allowed the garbage disposal to consume. The store offered three different quality levels of the product. The so-called "good" version was made of plastic but cost only ninety-four cents. The [again so-called] "better" product was made out of a light grade aluminum and costs two dollars and fifty cents. The "best" offering had a price tag of five dollars and ninety-four cents but had the feel that it would give any garbage disposal a run for its money. Would you dare venture to guess which ones I brought home? If you said the "best," you would be correct. Yet, they cost more than six times the amount of the entry-level style. Why would I pay over six times the amount for a product that fulfills the same role as the cheaper one? No, it is not because I have more money than I do sense; it is because *quality never grows old.*

"Quality is the result of pride."

Quality is the result of pride. If a company, or one of its employees, does not care about the quality of the product, it will end up being an inferior product. Quality is always the result of detailed planning and never an accident. Workers must be held responsible for the quality of their work and be rewarded when they produce excellence. Quality can never be forgotten, lest it soon be found in the enemy's camp.

If a competitor can offer an equal quality product at a lower price, you owe it to yourself, and to your customers, to find out how they do it. It could be the result of the competition being willing to live with less margin, or it could be that they are wiser in their purchasing and manufacturing techniques. Whatever the reason, you need to know. If it ends up being greed on your behalf, shame on you. If it happens to be that they are wiser, shame on you again.

The deciding factor for quality is less dependent on what goes into a product or service, than on what the consumer gets out of it. If a customer can buy a product with a very competitive price that fulfills his expectations, he or she will consider it as quality. When it comes to quality, you normally get what you pay for. I remember an old saying that goes something like this; *"If you want good clean oats expect to pay a fair price. However, if you can be satisfied with those that have made a one-way trip through a horse, now those come a bit cheaper."*

If you are not willing to sign your name to your work, then something tells me that the quality may be less than what it should be. We must remember that quality applies to people as well as to products. Make sure the level of your work will pass final inspection. The quality of your life will be closely related to the quality of your work. If a worker would make every product as if he were going to purchase it, he would be more concerned with quality.

A woman from Houston was driving through a small town in Utah when she noticed a sign advertising $5 haircuts. She wondered how anyone could offer such a low price, until she read the sign on a nearby salon that summed it up very well. It read, "We repair $5 haircuts!" A company built on price alone will soon find the cost of doing business to be more than it can withstand.

We must always be concerned with trying to improve the quality of our product or service, because if we do not, someone else will. A state of satisfaction, and an unwillingness to change, leads to obsolescence. If quality is not an overall goal of a company, the business will not survive for long. In addition, when cost reduction becomes the top priority, you can be assured that quality is going to suffer.

"Quality control" should mean more than simply the rejection of defective product; it should also mean taking the necessary steps to ensure quality the next time. Quality is not established by a one-time event but through repeat performances. It is the result of careful planning and wise choices. Quality must be built into a product and not offered as an option.

"If quality is not an overall goal of a company, the business will not survive for long."

I once read a sign in a repair shop that made a lot of sense. *"We offer three types of jobs: Cheap, quick and good. You may choose a combination of any two of these. However, you need to understand that a good quick job will not be cheap. A good job cheap won't be quick. A cheap job quick will not be good."* The speed of a task will long be forgotten, but the quality of it will be remembered forever.

Being in the sales profession, it has always been my philosophy that, *"You can shear a sheep many times, but you can only skin it once."* If I take unfair advantage of a customer, I will most likely only get one opportunity to do business with them. However, if I offer a quality service at a fair price, and do it with integrity, other orders will follow. A quality product or service warrants repeat customers. Quality will stand up through the passing of time, while inferior ones do a disappearing act. You may ask why, and I would simply say it is because *quality never grows old.*

*****

"May our Lord Jesus Christ himself and God our Father, who loved us and by his grace gave us eternal encouragement and good hope, encourage your hearts and strengthen you in every good deed and word." [2 Thessalonians 2:16-17]

34 - Who is Responsible for This?

I hate to admit it, but normally when I hear the question, "Who is responsible for this?" I am expecting someone to "catch the devil" so to speak, for something that has taken place. And more times than not, my fear of being found out causes me to remain silent. However, if I think there could possibly be some praise or credit involved, I almost throw my arm out of socket trying to get it in the air. The fact is, if we are going to share in the credit, we must be willing to share in the responsibility as well. However, to always take the blame and never share the fame makes us little more than a slave. It is a fact that you and I are responsible for our own responsibility.

Responsibility should increase the size of the heart and not the head. An increased level of responsibility will soon show you what a person is made of. The higher up the ladder of success you climb, the more responsibility you find!

"Responsibility should increase the size of the heart and not the head."

Perhaps nothing is more wasteful than burying one's talents. Keep them alive and well by accepting responsibility for becoming all you were designed to be. Many times people feel like they have done their part by carrying a chip on their shoulders. Each of us must accept responsibility for our own lot in life. If our neighbor's grass looks greener, it could be that he has been taking better care of it.

Most people are more concerned about their rights than their responsibilities. We must understand that you cannot have one without the other. On life's scales, there must be a balance. To shun responsibility is to turn your nose up at life.

A good name can soon become tarnished if the owner falls short of meeting his/her responsibilities. To the best of my research, Mr. Anonymous was the author of, *"No individual raindrop ever considers itself responsible for the flood."* However, we know that the person who shirks one's responsibility is a "drop-out" in life's terms. To begin preparing for future responsibilities simply means to take care of the ones you have now. To shirk today's responsibilities makes tomorrow's load unbearable.

We should be careful not to place responsibility on a person who has not proven themselves responsible - to do so is to set them up for failure.

If each person would merely accept his or her fair share of the load of responsibility, life would have fewer problems for everyone. If you turn your back on responsibility, you turn your back on humanity. You are responsible not only for your own life, but, to a degree, for all of the lives in your realm of influence.

It is our responsibility to answer the door when opportunity knocks. However, we must realize that with every opportunity comes a responsibility.

"With every opportunity comes a responsibility."

To leave a job half-done is but a bit better than never starting. For if someone else has to finish it, they will spend as much time trying to figure out what you have done, and why you did it, as they will in completing it. To accept responsibility is to fulfill your duty.

Opportunity normally does not come to you served on a silver platter. Usually you will find it on the cafeteria line, and you must help yourself. While you are at it, why not take a second helping? You are going to be blamed for it anyway!

*****

"...From everyone who has been given much, much will be demanded; and from the one who has been entrusted with much, much more will be asked." [Luke 12:48b]

35 - The Trio of Me, Myself and I

We do not have to look far to see the selfishness that exists in the world today. In fact, if most of us would like to get a close-up view to see what it really looks like, we simply need to take a glance in the mirror. Selfishness is something that most of us battle each and every day of our lives. Our society today tries its best to get us to buy into the lie that we are the axis upon which the world turns. If there is one song that comes close to telling it like it is, it is the one by Toby Keith entitled, ***"I Wanna Talk About Me."*** We may not want to admit it, but this is often exactly the way we feel. We cannot wait to bring *"The Trio of Me, Myself and I"* onto stage for our performance. However, when this happens, we may discover that the only one clapping is - you guessed it - me, myself and I.

The world constantly tells us that we need to look out for No. 1, but it needs to do a better job of letting us know that 'we' are not always going to be in that position. It would behoove us to give ourselves regular check-ups to make sure we are not affected with "I" problems, for when we are, we cannot see the needs of others.

It used to be when you heard someone saying, "Me, me, me, me, me, me, me, me!" it meant that he or she was preparing to sing. Not so today, for this is just the normal mode of conversation. It has been shown again and again that a person who is full of self leads an empty life. We must be willing to reach out to the needs of others to live a full rewarding life ourself. "Self" is a dirty four-letter word, and one we use without giving much thought. If we want our children to grow up to become a well-rounded person, we must teach them at an early age how to be unselfish; put the wants and needs of others in front of their own. To have the hope of happiness, a person must turn their thoughts outward beyond the self. How much more pleasant the world would be if each of us could be as generous and loving as we wish our neighbors to be. If we have hopes of changing the world, we must first change ourselves. The world does not think too much of the person who thinks too much of self.

"To have the hope of happiness, a person must turn their thoughts outward."

Cross-examine any trouble in your life, and you will discover "U" is in the middle of each one. Most would agree that we are usually our own worst enemy, and our problems are often the result of self-inflicted wounds. When we begin to blame others for our circumstances, we are only being selfish and not wanting to face the facts. Along the same line, every sin has "I" at the heart of it. Many times, I have tried to come up with even one sin that was not the direct result of selfishness, and, to this date, I have not been able to do so. It makes no difference which sin you look at, it was brought on by a person being wrapped up in self, blinded to the reality of what the consequences might be.

I have heard that a person who is wrapped up in themselves will make for a very small package, and I think it's true. If you will take the time to consider acts of selfishness, you will discover they are always standing in the receiving line, not in the serving line.

One of Teddy Roosevelt's children said of their father, *"He always wanted to be the bride at every wedding and the corpse at every funeral."* Some people just are not happy unless they are in the spotlight and the attention of the crowd is on them. It is a healthy thing to have a good self-image, but when it gets to the point where you think it's all about you, then it's not healthy. We must inoculate our self against the germ of conceit, for it will make everyone we are exposed to sick, and we will be the only one feeling fine. Even then, not for long.

"To get others to respect us, we must first show respect for others."

To get others to respect us, we must first show respect for others. To think only of self is a sure-fire way to be miserable. Selfishness pays no dividends, but the rewards of unselfishness are never ending. Many people will try to make others miserable when things are not going the way they want. However, we must realize that we cannot make our light shine any brighter by putting out another's.

Most would define a "bore" as someone who will not stop talking about him or herself long enough for us to talk. The majority of people who are listening to another are more concerned about what they are going to say next than they are about what is being said to them. We need to understand that it is not so much that others are against us; it is just that they are for themselves, first and foremost.

If you would stop and think about it, selfishness has less to do with living as one wishes to live, and more in wanting others to live as you wish them to. Again, the thoughts center on self, and the wants that possess it.

In closing, *"The trio of me, myself and I"* would like to sing a little song for you. However, before we do, we need to prepare our voices so you will be most impressed. Excuse us, if you will, while we get ready. "Me, me, me, me, me, me, me, me!"

*****

Then he said to them all: "If anyone would come after me, he must deny himself and take up his cross daily and follow me. For whoever wants to save his life will lose it, but whoever loses his life for me will save it." [Luke 9:23-24]

36 - It's Never Been This Late Before!

Very few statements are always true. But one of my favorites has become, *"It's never been this late before!"* For when you stop to think about it, there is not an ounce of falsehood in it. In each of our lives, we are closer to the end than at any other point before. If we could remember this and the truth it holds, we would be much more mindful in how we use our time. I believe we would spend more time making sure our priorities are what they should be, and that we are making the most of every minute of every day.

So many of us have a tendency to major in the minors and minor in the majors, when it should be the other way around. Any lack of time is an obvious result of unwise priorities, because time plays no favorite in the realm of daily life. We receive exactly the same number of hours and minutes every day. It doesn't matter how much money you have, you cannot buy an extra hour or two. Time is not for sale - it is truly a gift! We must accept it as such, and learn to use it wisely by choosing and setting our priorities in a proper manner. The next time somebody asks, "What time is it?" you can answer, "I don't know, but *it has never been this late before!"*

"Time is not for sale, it is truly a gift!"

Being good stewards of our time requires self-discipline. We must realize that killing time is like committing suicide, as time wasted can never be recaptured. Time thrown away can not be recycled. Not until we come to understand that our time on earth is limited will we learn to live each day to its fullest. We have a tendency to allow our time to be consumed with "busyness" when we should be developing relationships.

We must learn to manage our time. We can make it work for us or against us. Time management is the number one factor in determining whether a person will be a success or a failure, in both personal and business life.

Benjamin Franklin once said about time, *"If we lose our money, it gives us great concern. If we are cheated or robbed of it, we are angry. But money lost can be found; what we are robbed of may be restored. The treasure of our time, once lost, can never be recovered; yet we squander it as though it was nothing of worth or we had no use of it."* Oh, how much more should we be concerned about the spending of our time, rather than our money?

Time seems to fly by, but we need to remember that we are the pilot who decides where it goes. Life exists in the realm of time; to waste it is to throw life to the wayside. The more fully we understand the true value of time, the more we tend to take hold of each minute and enjoy it to its fullest. Laziness and procrastination are of no use. The longer we live, the more we comprehend how truly short life is. We make it shorter by carelessly wasting the time we do have.

"Time seems to fly by, but we must remember that we are the pilot that decides where it goes."

Life today is lived at a faster pace than in previous times, but it will be nothing compared to the speed of the future. We speed up everything to try and save time. However, we must realize that time cannot be saved, and what is not spent will be forever lost. We have a tendency to remember the things of the past as being more pleasant than they really were, and visualizing things at hand as being worse than they really are. We owe it to ourselves to get a proper perspective on both, and treat each moment as the miraculous gift it really is.

I believe television and video games are two of the greatest wasters of time in the lives of young people today. Just think of the unproductive hours that are wasted each day just on these two pastimes. (I almost used the word "activities" to describe them, but realized it would be wrong to refer to either as any such thing.) On second thought, don't think about the time wasted, because it might make you sick.

Margaret B. Johnstone once remarked, *"Time is a fixed income and, as with any income, the real problem facing most of us is how to live successfully within our daily allotment."* Time used for the betterment of humanity is never ill- spent but is invested with tremendous dividends. Each of us should strive to leave something behind that will stand strong against the erosion of time.

"*Time used for the betterment of humanity is never ill spent, but is invested with tremendous dividends.*"

A number of experts from different walks of life were once asked how much time they believed was needed for accomplishing the necessary activities in daily life - eating, sleeping, working, exercise, family time, and so on. When all the time allotments were totaled, the experts agreed that to accomplish everything, the average person would need forty plus hours each **day**. Is it any wonder that we are always tired then and way behind schedule? We can forget about the forty-hour week and start working on the forty-hour day! Having the gift of realizing how much time to devote to the different activities of each day and keeping it all in proper balance is a blessing indeed.

Leo Buscaglia once said, *"Time has no meaning in itself unless we choose to give it significance."* Nothing should be looked upon as a waste of time if the experience gained is used wisely.

A statement by Jonathan Edwards merits repeating: *"I resolve to live with all my might while I do live. I resolve never to lose one moment of time and to improve my use of time in the most profitable way I possibly can. I resolve never to do anything I wouldn't do, if it were the last hour of my life."* It is a fact that if we knew the hour our life clock was scheduled to stop, we would surely use the last hours in the way we knew to be the wisest. Why not start living that way right now? For we all know, *"It's never been this late before!"*

*****

"There is a time for everything, and a season for every activity under heaven: A time to be born and a time to die, a time to plant and a time to uproot, a time to kill and a time to heal, a time to tear down and a time to build, a time to weep and a time to laugh, a time to mourn and a time to dance..."
[Ecclesiastes 3:1-4]

37 - But You Don't Understand

The world would be a much more loving and caring place if we would first exert the effort to understand others before passing judgment on them. Actually, we shouldn't pass judgment. All of us have the desire to be understood, but far more important in the realm of living is to understand first. I am sure that I am not alone in the fact that I have jumped to conclusions before I really knew what was taking place and ended up making a complete fool out of myself. We all have a tendency to base judgments on what we perceive as the truth, rather than doing what we can to fully understand the facts. This does nothing but lead to trouble.

To cultivate understanding, you must be willing and have a tendency to seeing things as others see them, for in so doing, your perspective will change. So the next time you find yourself in the position of not agreeing with someone, and they say, *"But you don't understand...,"* please do yourself and others a favor and understand that you probably do not. You should try your best to allow them to enlighten you with the "truth," as they see it. Notice I said, *"As they see it,"* because they, too, may have a need for more information on which to base their final answer.

"To let someone know you understand is to let someone know he or she is loved."

To let someone know you understand is to let someone know he or she is loved. Empathy is the ability to understand why another sees things the way they do, and it plays a major role in building relationships. Before I can understand you, I must have a desire to do so. For if I have no want to understand, I will make a hasty decision and not give it a second thought, even though my reaction may be very inappropriate. We must be willing to put our feelings temporarily on hold, allowing us the chance to gather the necessary information to enable us to react wisely. The gathering of facts can do much in leading to understanding. We have an inherent need to be understood, but so does everybody else. To lighten the load of another, show some understanding.

"To lighten the load of another, show some understanding."

Sometimes having the nerve to admit misunderstanding will lead to understanding. If we are not too proud to let another know that we need more information before we decide on something, we will make wiser decisions. Sometimes we will not fully understand until we find ourselves at the point of admitting that we do not know it all. If our final understanding is based on knowledge, we are wise. Understanding has much to do with being able to lay aside preconceived ideas and seeing things for what they really are. To not understand is to draw false conclusions. Understanding cannot be taught but must be learned through the experiences of dealing with others. To understand something from a new perspective is to broaden our horizon and prevents us from being short sighted. It is necessary for everyone to understand that, contrary to our belief, others do not see us the same as we see ourselves, and they do not always see things the same way we do. How disheartening it is to argue with a person who understands what they are talking about!

We need to take hearsay with a grain of salt, and season it instead with the sweetness of understanding. Walking hand in hand will enable us to see eye-to-eye. We can squelch the urge to put others in their place by putting ourselves in their place instead. People are pleased when they know they are understood. Peace and happiness happen when understanding happens. An old German proverb states, *"To understand and be understood makes our happiness on earth."* The need for understanding is as necessary for sustaining life as food and water.

For those of us who are plagued with fear, we need to know that fear will be erased through understanding. The majority of the times we allow fear to enter into our minds, it is because we do not know and understand enough about the situation. Learn more.

We can enjoy things without understanding them, but our joy will be deepened with every ounce of gained insight. To love or hate someone, or something, without first understanding, is a mistake that has no rival. Understanding comes more from hindsight than it does from foresight. For many times when we take the chance to look back at something and try to gain understanding, we can see with a vision, a truth that we were blinded to before.

There will always be employment for one who works at understanding others. Good listeners are not only popular, they actually grow to understand others. To understand is to offer great assistance to another. Do yourself a favor and vow never to allow the fact that you don't understand someone to prevent you from getting to know them, and thus understanding them. A tear in the eye of another can be dried with the towel of understanding. If we truly know the sufferings of another, it is much easier to suffer with them.

> **"There will always be employment for the one who works at understanding others."**

It has been said that only a fool would vote for, or against, something they do not understand. Hatred is a sure sign of not understanding what is going on, and a prime example of what it takes to make one a fool. However, we must understand that loving without first understanding can be quite foolish as well.

It is OK not to agree with everyone, but we should at least make an effort to try to understand why he or she believes what they do. And it is also good advice not to laugh at another until you first understand why they are laughing at themselves. For just as sure as you do, you will hear someone say, *"But you don't understand."*

*****

"Have you understood all these things?" Jesus asked. "Yes," they replied. [Matthew 13:51]

38 - Who Gives A Hoot?

⌣∴∽

"Who gives a hoot?" you might ask. Evidently, the owl does, because that is about all he ever seems to do, yet he earns the title of "wise." So maybe we need to start giving a hoot as well. I am not exactly sure how "Mr. Give-A-Hoot" first received the honor of being the owner of such a prized possession as wisdom, but it might have something to do with the fact that when he speaks, he is always asking a question, "Who?" It is a truth that you will grow more toward wisdom when you ask questions than when you simply share information that you already know.

A couple of years ago while vacationing in England, I found a flip chart of different sayings, which they called "Mature Insights." I am not sure what buying a flip chart of mature insights says about me personally, but I like to think it was because of my being a prudent student of life, and I wanted to see if there happened to be some with which I was not familiar. Well, one of the first ones that I flipped to was, *"Wisdom comes with age - Sometimes age comes alone!"* What I want to know is, "Who told them about me?"

It is true that wisdom is usually associated with years, but occasionally you will discover young people who understand truths that even the elderly have missed. I have been fortunate to have met and become acquainted with more than a few who I consider to be in this elite group. I won't mention any names, but if you are thinking that you might be one of them, well, you probably aren't.

"Knowledge, unless chaperoned by wisdom, will soon be called a fool."

Wisdom is, or at least should be, the by-product of experiencing life. To have traveled through life and missed it could very well be evidence that you were asleep at the wheel. Knowledge, unless chaperoned by wisdom, will soon be called a fool.

To hear wisdom from others is but a shadow of what you gather from first hand experience. For to live through wisdom makes it real and usable. To hear it from others is but a fable. It is like hearing of a far-away country in your studies and having an assurance that it actually exists. However, the first step you take in that distant land is what makes it real for you. All the words ever written about wisdom pale in comparison to even one first-hand experience.

An old Chinese proverb goes like this: *"I hear and I forget. I see and I remember. I do and I understand."* Each in itself is a necessary step toward wisdom.

Wisdom is refined by the fires of experience. Only those who can stand the heat will know the joy of being part owner of the world of wisdom.

Knowledge and wisdom are often mistaken as equals. This is far from the truth, for where both are found, wisdom will be the boss every time, knowledge the common laborer. A wise person is one who is willing to learn from all others, no matter their gender, age or nationality.

"Wisdom is refined by the fires of experience."

A person called "wise" who has not love toward others is far from living up to his name. Love, when allowed to make others feel important, will make great strides in convincing them of your wisdom.

To be wise is to learn from the mistakes of others as well as your own. Time passes much too quickly to experience each mistake personally. A wise man uses his ears more than his mouth, a fool just the opposite. Wisdom *may* be the reward you receive for listening when you would much prefer talking. It is just however, a possibility, not a guarantee. Wisdom talks less and says more!

"Wisdom talks less and says more!"

True wisdom will not be forgotten but will become a part of all your beliefs and actions. It will penetrate and change you from the inside out. Wisdom consists in collecting the jewels of each day and wearing them on your thinking cap. After you have claimed wisdom as your own, you should then concentrate on finding ways to share the benefits of it with others, for it is not a treasure to be hoarded. Wisdom without truth is not wisdom at all, but "fools gold"!

*****

"Blessed is the man who finds wisdom, the man who gains understanding, for she is more profitable than silver and yields better returns than gold. She is more precious than rubies; nothing can compare with her." [Proverbs 3:13-15]

39 - Work Is Not A Dirty Four-Letter Word

Have you ever known someone who worked harder to get out of work than they would have if they had just tackled the task at hand? Some people act as if work is beneath them, and they will do whatever it takes to avoid it. We would be appalled if we knew the billions of dollars that are wasted in a year's time in our country alone from workers who give less than what they should while on the clock. When you stop to think about it, not giving your all to the job you are being paid to do is no more than another form of stealing. Yet most who are not willing to give their all would never think of taking something that did not belong to them.

I think it's time for a wake-up call, and time to understand that if we are not willing to do our job, then we need to step aside for someone who is. Laziness seems to be the norm rather than the exception when it comes to the average worker today. Robert Half said, *"Laziness is a secret ingredient that goes into failure. But it's only kept a secret from the person who fails."* Understand that it is never a disgrace to work for a living. Make sure your work is not a disgrace to your life. Work should be a soothing ointment, not a bitter pill. As radio personality Earl Pitts might say, "Wake up America! *Work is not a dirty four-letter word!*"

"We need to go to work and make our own luck."

If we sit around waiting for luck to come knocking on our door, chances are we will be sitting for a while. We need to go to work and make our own luck. The only time your job should be viewed as "work" is if there were something else you would rather be doing. A job that brings pleasure should be counted as joy. When it becomes a duty, count it as curse. Shame on anyone for keeping a job they do not enjoy for longer than six months. When a worker is not matched with something that allows him to take pride and feel good about his accomplishments, and enjoy what he is doing, then he is doing himself a huge disfavor by continuing. However, when a person has a job he loves, and it's a good match with his skills, you can be assured the product he produces will be of utmost quality. Do what you like, and like what you do!

No sleeping pill can offer a night's rest equal to the one that comes after a good day's work, and the feeling of accomplishment is simply a bonus. Each of us should put our whole self into our work and give it all we've got. Rather than killing time, we should work it to death. If we do that, everyone will benefit. In all my research, I could not find even one death certificate that lists the reason for death as "drowning in sweat."

I read somewhere that the recipe for getting to the top of the ladder is to get up early, put in a good day's work, and marry the boss's daughter! The only problem with that is the boss does not have enough daughters for everyone, so most of us are just going to have to rely on the first two steps and hope someone important is watching. Oh yes, for your information, it has been found to be impossible to climb the ladder of success while sitting down. However, it is a fact that there are two known ways to get to the top of an oak tree; one is to get busy and climb it; the other is to sit on an acorn and wait. I wish you Godspeed!

"Rather than killing time, we should work it to death."

Most workers are capable of doing more than they think they can, but, in reality, most do less than what they think they do. Many people have a wishbone where the backbone is supposed to be. No formula for success will work unless you do. Anyone who does only what is required of him is a slave, and he does not become free until he does more than the minimum. Promotions go to the one who is willing to do more than what is necessary to get by.

Like it or not, your work will speak for itself; make sure what it says will make you proud! The job you perform should be your masterpiece, and one to which you proudly sign your name. Work that is done properly actually gives life to life! When we come to the realization that the world doesn't owe us a living, and start earning our own way, everyone wins. Do the job expected of you without whining, and do a little extra, again without comment, and soon you will be recognized for your contribution.

One word of warning though in regard to getting to the point of believing you are so important that your place of employment could not do without you. If this should ever happen to you, draw a bucket of water, stick your arm in, withdraw it, and notice the hole you have left. Now dry your arm off, and realize that no one is irreplaceable!

"...no one is irreplaceable!"

Many people dream of working hard and finally getting to a position where they can hire other people to do the job they were hired to do. In other words, they want to be an executive. But my advice for you is that if you want a position where you can lay around all day and still produce results, become a chicken.

A Chinese rhyme goes like this; *"This one makes a net; this one stands and wishes. Would you like to bet which one catches the fishes?"* I think we all know the answer to that one. Elbow grease is what keeps industry moving freely. And don't worry; it doesn't leave a stain on your clothes. Whatever it is you are called to do, do it as if you were doing it for yourself, because ultimately you are. If you don't remember anything else, remember this: *"Work is not a dirty four-letter word!"*

*****

"Serve wholeheartedly, as if you were serving the Lord, not men, because you know that the Lord will reward everyone for whatever good he does, whether he is a slave or free." [Ephesians 6:7-8]

40 - Worry Wart

The story is told of a businessman who had always been a worrier, so much so that he was plagued with ulcers. One day he ran into a doctor friend who asked about his health. The businessman replied, "My health is fine. My ulcers are gone, and I don't have a worry in the world!" The doctor replied, "Wow! How did you manage that?" The businessman said, "I decided to hire myself a professional worrier to do all of my worrying for me." This got the full interest of the doctor, as he himself struggled with worry. He asked, "How much does something like that cost?" The businessman replied, "I pay him $150,000 a year." The doctor's first question was, "How in the world can you afford to pay him that much?" His friend smiled and said, "I don't know. I let him worry about that!"

Wouldn't it be nice if we could actually hire someone to take care of our worrying for us? My mother was one of the most experienced worriers I have ever met. If there wasn't something to worry about, she would worry for what might be coming next. If ever the title of *"Worry Wart"* was appropriate, she would have been in the running.

Arthur Somers Roche is credited with what I think is one of the best insights on the subject of worry: *"Worry is a tiny stream of fear trickling through the mind. If encour-*

aged, it cuts a channel into which all other thoughts are drained." The bad thing about that truth is that it doesn't take much encouragement for worry to take up permanent residence in our minds. When it does, danger follows. Worry robs one of their creative juices, and leaves the mouth, heart and head dry as a bone.

"Worry has a knack for making our faith second guess itself."

Worry has a way of making us believe that tomorrow will hold more of today's troubles, when in reality our troubles of today may already be gone. Worry can make our faith second-guess itself. In reality, worry is a waste of time and a trademark of fools.

If we allow the fear of trouble to take over our thoughts, we can be assured of one thing: time being wasted! Worry is the venom that poisons our dreams. It can snatch us from flight and happiness and cause us to slither in sorrow. Hope is as right as worry is wrong.

Worry has a way of convincing otherwise wise men and women that they need to waste time fretting over frivolous matters. Worry and despair ruin lives that were meant to be productive, and they bring the weight of burdens we were never meant to carry. Worry is nothing more than hope that has been starved to death. We have the choice of which one gets fed, our worries or our hopes. Hope will grow into a helping hand while worry becomes a stumbling stone.

Evan Esar once said, *"Worry is like a rocking chair: It gives you something to do, but it doesn't get you anywhere."* It's true! Worry gets you nowhere, and wears you out on the way!

The formula for making life miserable is to worry about tomorrow. Worry is the greatest waster of time, and makes misery of the moment. Most worries never show themselves, but their shadows steal the sunshine. The imagining of future trouble has thrown many under the wheels of worry and woe.

Worry can take our thinking on trails we would never consider on our own. And we will often find that when hope is put to bed, worry is up and active. Worry is nothing more than slow death, and a telltale sign of one who may be losing control of sanity. Life is too short to worry about washing the windows before you see dirt.

Anais Nin once said, *"Anxiety is love's greatest killer. It makes one feel as you might when a drowning man holds onto you. You want to save him, but you know he will strangle* you *in the panic."* Worry does have a way of choking the life out of you, and may make you want to give up on living. It is a waster of time and a slayer of dreams.

In regard to work, the easiest of tasks become troublesome toil when worry gets its way. If you find worry following you to your job, work it to death!

When we can train ourselves to tackle one step at a time, trouble cannot overtake us. And if you should find yourself being hounded by the dogs of despair, why not just hire yourself a professional worrier, and let him be the one who gets bit!

*****

"Therefore I tell you, do not worry about your life, what you will eat or drink; or about your body, what you will wear. Is not life more important than food, and the body more important than clothes? Look at the birds of the air; they do not sow or reap or store away in barns, and yet your heavenly Father feeds them. Are you not much more valuable than they? Who of you by worrying can add a single hour to his life?" [Matthew 6:25-27]

Printed in the United States
205699BV00001B/1-165/P